THE
MONEY
MESSIAH$

THE MONEY MESSIAH$

Norman King

Coward-McCann, Inc.
New York

Designed by Richard Oriolo

Library of Congress Cataloging in Publication Data

King, Norman, date.
The money messiahs.
1. Investment advisers—Biography.   2. Capitalists
and financiers—Biography.   I. Title.
HG4621.K5 1983   332.6'2 [B]   83-5265
ISBN 0-698-11132-X

Printed in the United States of America

Cariño—
Je t'aime ma chérie

Contents

THE
MONEY
MESSIAH$

1
Eliot Janeway

Although Eliot Janeway sees himself as a "muscular optimist" in regard to the American economy, most of his fellow economists and followers feel that he is basically pessimistic. Many equate him with that large and growing number of today's investment counselors whom the media lump together under the catch-all term "the doom-and-gloom boys."

And yet Janeway is a familiar figure on lecture platforms throughout the country. He appears on radio and television talk shows as a guest with financial know-how and money-management advice for individuals. He produces two financial newsletters through a well-coordinated staff of a dozen-odd employees in New York. One newsletter is a weekly advisory with a circulation of about 5,000; the other is a detailed commentary in the form of a consultation service with a more exclusive circulation of perhaps 1,500. For many years he wrote a daily syndicated newspaper column for the Chicago Tribune–New York News Syndicate.

Eliot Janeway started out as an economist, and was reading trends in the national economy as far back as the 1930s, publishing his thoughts on finance from both a business and personal standpoint.

Trained in economics at the height of the 1920s boom, he observed first-hand the Market Crash of 1929 and lived through the subsequent Great Depression that followed, watching it settling over the entire world to paralyze economies everywhere and frustrate learned men in all attempts to revive them.

He witnessed the complete reversal of economic practice in government when Franklin D. Roosevelt followed the advice of his mentors and espoused the revolutionary theories of John Maynard Keynes to involve the United States in deficit spending to stimulate the laggard economy.

The economy managed to revive itself in the 1940s, but it did so largely because of the intervention of World War II, which forced the industrial output into high gear to fight a war on two fronts. This fact was not lost on Janeway. As an economist, he was never a member of either of the two opposing schools: the monetarists and the Keynesians.

The monetarists hold that the key to a healthy economy is based strictly on the money *supply*, which expands or contracts in accordance with the interest rates set by the Federal Reserve Board. The Keynesians believe that there is less importance in the amount of money in existence than there is in the amount of money spent by the government in stimulating the economy and the amount taken back by the government in taxes to brake it.

Janeway found both philosophies restrictive and formula-ridden, and began studying the performance of the economy from the standpoint of an observer as well as a participant. He was appalled to find that there were no tools available by which he could make determinations of business trends.

It was largely through his work with two men—Tom Corcoran and Ben Cohen—that the Budget Bureau was established in the White House through the Reorganization Act of 1938. The Bureau became the primary tool for measurement of economic conditions and has been used for that purpose ever since. The establishment of the Gross National Product as a belwether for determining the potency and direction of the economy was a direct outgrowth of the accounting system set up in the Budget Bureau.

Today Janeway is hardly sanguine about the GNP in forecasting trends. "The analyst relying on the GNP numbers to discern the underlying economic trend, or the financial soundness of the American economy today, is in the position of a bystander at a grade crossing watching a freight train go by. Recording the numbers on the boxcars will not shed any light on either the freight inside any car or the destination of the train."

Eliot Janeway was born in New York City on January 1, 1913, the son of Meyer Joseph Janeway, a physician, and the former Fanny Siff. The New Year's Day baby grew up in New York City and attended Cornell University, graduating in 1932 with a B.A. in economics.

He took postgraduate courses in his primary interest at the London School of Economics and then returned to the United States to look for a job. By now the Great Depression had made job-hunting an almost futile exercise for thousands of graduates. Janeway continued with his graduate studies, hoping a job opportunity would open. He also began writing articles on various subjects on a free-lance basis, selling them to magazines and newspapers.

One of his job prospects, McGraw-Hill, wanted to take him on, but the company had instituted a freeze on hiring. His interviewer recommended him to A. W. Zelomek, an economist recognized as the best in the consumer field. Hopeful and optimistic, Janeway went to an interview and convinced Zelomek that he had learned the field well enough to work for him.

"Your broad international background would bring me exactly the new perspective on the international commodity markets that we need in our work," he told Janeway. "But we couldn't begin to afford you. With your educational qualifications, I wouldn't feel right offering you less than thirty-five dollars a week."

And, he went on to explain, he simply could not afford to pay that.

"What would you think of my working mornings—for twenty-one dollars a week?" asked Janeway.

Zelomek smiled. "You've got a deal—but for six mornings a week. Saturdays too!"

Janeway worked for and learned from Zelomek for several years, and then heard of an opening at Henry Luce's Time, Inc. As Janeway later told it, Luce's publications were enjoying record advertising commitments from the best-rated corporations in the country. However, Time Magazine was being criticized in the board rooms of America for its somewhat amateurish approach to business and finance. And during the New Deal days, the public wanted to know more and more about the economy and the government's steps to regulate business.

"Time's business editor offered me $18,000 a year," Janeway recalled, "a lot of money in the world of 1938. I was only twenty-five, but I was already beginning to spread my by-line around. I countered with an offer to take $12,000 and write just two stories a week. I kept my independence, and both Time and I came out way ahead."

Janeway moved to Washington, where he could observe politics and finance first-hand, a particularly advantageous position during the excitement and theatrics of the New Deal. He spent much of his time free-lancing pieces on his own.

From 1937 to 1940, he worked as a part-time unofficial economic adviser to a freshman representative in Congress, a young Texan named Lyndon B. Johnson.

During his years in Washington, Janeway met and married Elizabeth Hall. The couple had two sons, Michael Charles and William Hall. Elizabeth Janeway went on to become a well-known novelist, critic, and leader in the women's liberation movement.

In 1940 Janeway was promoted to associate editor of Time and moved his family back to New York to work on the weekly newsmagazine for two years. But he kept up his free-lance writing.

It was during the pre-war years that he worked on a book-length writing project. He collaborated with Edmund Taylor and Edgar Snow on *Smashing Hitler's International; the Strategy of a Political Offensive Against the Axis.* The book was published in 1941, before America had any idea it would soon be involved in fighting the Third Reich.

Once the United States entered the worldwide conflict, Janeway was kept busy as *Time* expanded its staff to report on the war and stepped up its coverage of politics, sociology, and the human ramifications of the struggle. Within a year, Janeway was appointed economic adviser to the editor-in-chief of Time, Inc. He served in that capacity for two years.

The war was beginning to wind down in 1944 when *Newsweek* approached Janeway to lure him away from the Luce organization. The rival publication wanted him to serve as a consultant on business trends. Janeway continued to relish his freedom as well as his ability to make it on his own. He worked out a deal that allowed him considerable free-lance writing time, thus gaining independence from the more confining job of editing from a desk.

His specialty was analysis of the management of the war. His work with Taylor and Snow had given him a good working relationship with reporters who had been in the field and who had piqued his interst in the daily mechanics of armed combat. Military articles on the various aspects of the war for *Time, Life,* and *Fortune* inspired him to put together a behind-the-scenes book on World War II, not chronicling the more or less predictable story of the action on the various fronts, but telling the story of the economic problems faced by the Roosevelt Administration in the mobilization of the entire country during the years of fighting. According to Janeway, the solutions of the various crises had produced experiments in a "new economics," and had molded a kind of "politics of crisis" as a by-product of the economics of mobilization.

Janeway admired Roosevelt's wartime efforts and featured them prominently in the book. He became fascinated by the inextricable link between the American economy and the technology that made the war machine run. These fascinations were projected as a story of the past, *The Struggle for Survival*, which appeared in 1951, published by the Yale University Press Chronicles of America under the editorship of Janeway's colleague, Allan Nevins. It was later reissued by Weybright and Talley. It was Janeway's first book written under his own by-line.

Coincidentally, when *Struggle for Survival* was published, America was once again at war, this time in Korea. That fact made Janeway's thesis—that the economy and the war were solidly linked—all the more viable. He recognized that the breakdown in the economy during the 1930s had been neutralized to a large degree by the advent of World War II—it had not been cured by Keynesian fiscal policies, as FDR's apologists (those who were Keynesians themselves) loved to assert.

"With the economy on a war footing for a second time within a decade," Janeway wrote, "the Administration began to project a plan to build a permanent base for war production into the economy."

The Korean conflict dragged on for many long months without solution; its seeming endlessness propelled Dwight D. Eisenhower into the White House. After his visit to Korea a truce was effected, which unfortunately became nothing more than a podium for debate on Eastern and Western philosophies of government. But the shooting war was at last in abeyance.

After the end of World War II, Janeway's interest had turned once again to his first and only love—the economy. He had observed that America and the way it managed its financial problems had changed dramatically from what it was during his youth to what it was during the last days of the war.

"In 1946," he wrote, "the memory of wartime governmental management of the economy was still fresh in everyone's mind;

the economic revolution that started with Keynes's theories and Roosevelt's experiments had turned Washington's responsibility for full employment and prosperity from an emergency takeover into a peacetime commitment."

There was an increase in the public's interest in economics, aroused in many people who had never before expressed any desire to know how money worked and what its uses and abuses were. Janeway perceived a new role for himself, based to a degree on his earlier training in individual finance under his early mentor, A. W. Zelomek.

Janeway put his talents to work forecasting economic trends not only for business and industry but for the public as well. His medium of expression was not confined to one kind of publication. The time-tested method of getting his messages across to a wide audience had been a regularly appearing newspaper column, but the postwar world had taken to newsletters as well as periodicals, so Janeway determined to try both.

Newsletters had existed for some time in America—for example, the *Kiplinger Letter* from Washington had originated in the 1920s—but now they were becoming a finely tuned method of conveying important information quickly.

As a purveyor of restricted-interest information—like economic forecasting—the newspaper column had (and still has) several distinct disadvantages compared to the regularly published newsletter. Newspaper writing must be concise and hard-hitting, and space is limited to a particular number of words for each appearance. The information must be couched in general terms in order not to be misunderstood by the average reader. Newspapers reach many thousands of people not at all interested in the subject of a particular column, and the opposite is also true: they don't reach many large groups of people who might be interested in that same subject.

Newspapers employ a scattergun technique. They run stories appealing to the masses, to specific groups, and to isolated individuals: there is no attempt to address exclusively any particular segment of society. On the other hand, a newsletter can be selective and can be sent to specific readers interested in a particular subject. It can be expansive, detailed, and more precisely worded; it can be familiar, using special jargon, and doesn't have to assume the reader is an ignoramus. There is a feeling of intimacy, of confidentiality, a feeling of being on the inside that can be exploited in the writing style of the newsletter.

Janeway felt there were thousands of men and women who wanted to know more about the economy as it affected them directly. By writing a newspaper column, he got his message across to interested middle-class wage-earners who wanted to know how to manage money. Readers who, after reading his column, became interested in more technical and specific advice could then subscribe to his newsletter for detailed counseling.

The Janeway Publishing and Research Corporation was founded to take care of the publication of the newsletter, called at the time *The Janeway Service*, later renamed *The Janeway Letter*.

Forecasting stock market trends was far from a new skill at the time Janeway began his publishing company. From its inception, observers of the stock market had noticed that there were trends and cycles in the prices of common stocks, securities, and bonds.

Various devices had been used to trace and predict the swings in stock and bond prices. One of the earliest attempts to analyze the market was the Dow Jones Average, established in 1889 by Charles H. Dow and Edward Jones, the founding editors of *The Wall Street Journal*, which at that time was exclusively devoted to financial news.

They had observed that as a group, stocks tended to rise and fall together rather than separately. Even stock in a company that was ailing and losing ground financially would tend to gain value during a general uptrend.

Dow and Jones charted the prices on a graph. They then

gathered together stocks of comparable types of companies—for example, industrial corporations—and averaged them out. Their original industrial average included thirty different industrial stocks; it still does. The names of the companies changed occasionally, but most of them have remained the same over the years: Du Pont, General Motors, Procter & Gamble, Sears Roebuck, U.S. Steel.

Dow and Jones then added the selling prices in dollars of all the component stocks and divided that figure by a mathematical formula that was supposed to counterbalance the effects of dividends, stock splits, and other factors. The resulting figure became the Dow Jones Industrial Average (DJIA), the foremost indicator used in predicting market trends.

But Dow and Jones were also concerned with other groupings of stocks. They took twenty leading railroad stocks and averaged them out for the Dow Jones Rail Average. They did the same thing with the utilities, using fifteen utility stocks, for the Dow Jones Utility Average. Using all sixty-five of the above stocks, they then made up a composite average called the Dow Jones Composite Average.

Using these averages, the analysts then began studying the market as it rose and fell, charting each move up and down on a hunch basis. The up and down movements were likened to ocean waves and tides in the graph configurations. The tides were long-term trends—major bull markets (rising prices) or major bear markets (falling prices). They were called "primary" movements. Each lasted from about one to six years.

These long-term trends were interrupted periodically by the waves, or short-term rallies and dips, which lasted from a few weeks to one or more months. They were called "secondary" movements. And these two trends in turn were interrupted by ripples, lasting only several days. Ripples were deemed inconsequential.

Although the waves ebbed and flowed, the direction of the tide could be measured by marking the "sand" at the highest point reached by the waves. If they pushed beyond the mark, the tide was rising. When the highest wave fell short, the tide was usually reversing direction.

They found that there were several declines on the way to every advancing market. However, a major bull market trend would continue as long as each successive market advance went to a higher peak than the one preceding it, and each successive secondary reaction stopped at a higher bottom than the last.

The opposite was true. When each successive decline carried to a new low, and each interim rally ended at a point below the previous one, the bear market was said to be in effect.

One basic rule of the Dow Theory was that a primary movement in the Industrial Average was never established until there was a corroborating movement in the Rail Average. If the corroborating movement did not come, then the primary movement had to be discounted.

Often, after a long rise or decline, the fluctuations of the averages tended to remain within a narrow range. In other words, there would be no indication of whether or not the market was headed up or down. The theory was that this was an accumulation or distribution of stocks. Only when the average broke out on either upper side or lower side would it indicate a direction to be taken. In either case, the rail average had to corroborate.

This theory, called the Dow Theory, was the one that most stock market analysts were familiar with when Janeway came into the business. It had proved itself handsomely during the 1929–32 market decline, the 1933 turnup, and the 1937 bust.

The market swings during the 1937 decline proved to be a perfect example of the Dow Theory at work. From a high of 194.40 in March 1937, the Industrial Average slid off nearly 30 points to 165.51 in June and rallied to 190.20 two months later, short of the previous high. A dive to 164.39 passed the previous low and forecast a bear market. Then there was a 65-point drop of the market to a bottom of 98.95 in March 1938.

By World War II, other analysts were tinkering with the theory, although it was generally considered to be reliable. However, new men were coming in who thought they could refine the system, for it did not always work. New indicators were selected to test against the Dow, and methods of computing trends became more sophisticated.

The Dow Theory was basically a *technical* one, dependent on mathematics and statistics. Arrayed against the technicians was another breed of stock market advisers who espoused the *fundamental* theory of prediction. Suspicious of the Dow Theory because it held that stocks moved in a solid pack—but there were obviously times when certain stocks did *not* move with the pack—the fundamentalists tended to ignore price configurations and explored the individual worth and value of each company considered separately.

Furthermore, they believed that there were outside forces at work on the stock market that had nothing to do with the lines on the charts. Economic conditions in the nation at large—and in the rest of the world—and the situation in the business community all affected stock movements.

The technician thus based his or her investment decisions on a reading and interpretation of chart formations or compilations of statistics.

The fundamentalist based his or her decisions primarily on basics such as general economic conditions, supply and demand, labor problems, the nature of the product, earnings, and dividends.

Janeway brought a great many outside strengths with him to the field of market analysis. First of all, he hadn't been trained in any one specific type of analysis. Second, he had studied world conditions—economic, political, and sociological—and knew a great deal more about them than the average Wall Street technician.

But he harbored no preconceived prejudice against technicians. In fact, what he did was to combine his own fundamentalist approach with the best of the ongoing technical schools of analysis to develop his own individual advisory method.

The timing for Janeway's plunge into investment counseling could not have been more fortunate, for the postwar years were peculiarly adapted to the need for advice on investment in the U.S. economy.

It was a time of affluence for most Americans. The soldiers were back and were now at last working at peacetime jobs. There was plenty of money available for astute investment. Payrolls were generous, and prices had not yet escalated to the point of robbing the workers of their nice financial edge. The men and women who had stayed at home to build the war machine had been unable to buy consumer products during the war years. There was nothing to do with their money but salt it away in bank accounts for future use. And the future had finally arrived.

Stocks and bonds were quite properly the place to put that money. Janeway correctly saw that the postwar years would be prosperous ones, with a rising stock market that would continue to go up with increasing production and profits for American business.

However, he was one of the few economists who saw clearly that the market would not continue upward forever. He had observed, sometimes with admiration, sometimes with amusement, and sometimes with dismay the experiments initiated by FDR in his attempt to get the country out of the doldrums of the Depression.

He was bemused, as other economists were, by Roosevelt's move to devalue the dollar on January 1, 1934, pegging the cost of an ounce of gold at $35 an ounce, almost twice what it had been worth originally at $20.67. That meant in effect that the dollar in 1934 lost half its 1933 value. A 1933 dollar bought .05 ounce of gold; a 1934 dollar bought only .0286.

The stock market crash had resulted in a deflationary depression; that is, prices of goods were far lower than they had been in the 1920s. Roosevelt's idea in devaluing the dollar was to raise commodity prices by making the dollar worth less in relation to gold.

Worthy as it was, the scheme didn't work. What happened was that dollar devaluation attracted foreign gold to America. In exchange for his gold, a foreigner received more dollars per ounce, substantially increasing exports, because the foreign countries now had more dollars to spend, but accumulating three-fourths of the world's gold, for which the U.S. had little use.

Janeway was even more intrigued by Roosevelt's experiments with the public works projects advocated by Keynes. It was a dramatic shift in American policy, going full-tilt against the old American way.

Nevertheless, the economy still lagged, although there were spurts of activity. It was the approach of World War II, and America's sudden production boom resulting from foreign contracts for war materiel, that got the economy on its feet and stabilized the dollar.

"The failure of the New Deal to find a peacetime solution for unemployment simplified the economic side of the problem of war mobilization as much as the traumatic shock of Pearl Harbor had simplified the political side," Janeway wrote later.

Roosevelt kept prices within reason, thus limiting the effects of inflation. Even though there was an inflation after the end of the war, his earlier moves had deferred it by keeping the price curve flat. What Janeway noted about the war and the economy was that the country's prosperity was a combination of Roosevelt's mobilization policies *and* wartime production. Prosperity and the war could not be separated.

Later, when the postwar economy was flourishing, Janeway rued the "tacit acceptance of war, limited and recurrent, as a way of life," while admitting the benefits of military production. His one concern, voiced early in the postwar years, was that the economy would have to expand faster than the cost of the military machine, or that wage and price controls would have to be put in place to slow down the inflationary spiral once it began.

The American people were lucky. The postwar years did not produce a sudden spurt of inflation—one that did occur was rapidly defused by controls, which were soon lifted—nor did it produce a sudden deflationary spiral due to overproduction. Within five years, there was another war in the offing. Although the Korean conflict was not called a war, it did produce guns, tanks, airplanes, and other military hardware, and the economic pot continued to boil.

Janeway's outlook for the postwar years was bullish. And he continued to be optimistic all though the years of the Eisenhower prosperity, from 1952 to 1960.

Meanwhile, his newsletter and newspaper column had made him many friends in low and high places. Persons of influence and standing became his intimates, and for some of them he became a personal financial adviser. He had politicians, captains of industry, and movers and shakers of all stripes as clients.

His pronouncements on economics were heard with growing respect. With the country rolling along in unbounded prosperity, most people were making money too fast to concern themselves with the stock market—and those that did had a feeling that the market would continue rising and rising and rising—conceivably forever.

Lyndon B. Johnson, serving in Congress in the postwar years, was a great admirer of Janeway, particularly his writings on Roosevelt and the mobilization of the economy to fight World War II. Johnson was an instinctive financier; he understood economic developments at a gut-level comprehension that helped make him a perfect politician.

The two men got along well together. Janeway persuaded Johnson to run for President in 1956, when Eisenhower ran for reelection. Johnson didn't even get the nomination. Adlai Stevenson did—and lost.

However, when Johnson tried again in 1960, the Stevenson era was over. Janeway worked hard for his friend, raising funds for the campaign in the financial community. But Johnson's campaign efforts were insufficient to derail the Kennedy juggernaut. Kennedy became the Democratic candidate. Janeway was appalled; he didn't think Kennedy would make a good President. When Johnson agreed to become Kennedy's running mate, surprising and confounding all his and Kennedy's friends, Janeway was through. He was so outraged that he withdrew his support from the Democrats and threw it to Nixon.

However, when Johnson became President after Kennedy's assassination in 1963, Janeway rallied to the cause and supported him for a time. They had differences of opinion on fiscal policy, but the key point of their disagreement—the one that widened the rift between them and caused irreparable damage—was the management of the Vietnam War.

Ironically enough, it was because of these differences with Johnson that Janeway achieved a breakthrough with the public at large, which in turn enhanced his reputation in economic as well as political circles and made his name, if not a household word, at least recognizable to a broad cross-section of the American people.

American involvement in Vietnam began during the early part of the Kennedy Administration, when a few "observers" were sent there to bolster a tottering political regime that had been abandoned by the French pullout after Dienbienphu. By the end of 1963, at the time of Kennedy's assassination, there were over twenty thousand Americans in Vietnam.

Once Johnson was in office, he became fascinated with the Vietnam situation. It was his considered opinion that if enough Americans were involved, the Vietcong could be defeated and Vietnam saved from communism. Troops began pouring into the country. By December 31, 1966, there were 385,000 men in Vietnam, not including 60,000 in the U.S. fleet and another 33,000 stationed in Thailand.

Janeway was concerned about the economic effects of waging such a war. He had seen at close hand the high cost of mobilization of men and weaponry. He was not at all prone to condone communism; in fact, in the Cold War crises in Europe he was usually hawkish.

Now, however, he sensed a great deal of trouble for the economy. He rightly concluded that President Johnson had decided to try to wage war without paying for it—to produce both guns and butter, rather than guns or butter. Janeway believed there would be serious consequences if Johnson continued such a policy.

His first concern was the stock market. His second one— which proved to be of primary consideration later on—was inflation.

"My switch to pessimism about the stock market came in the autumn of 1965," Janeway wrote. "It was then that the financial consequences of Johnson's systematic escalation by stealth in Vietnam, budgeted by embezzlement, let loose the inflationary pressures which deflated first the bond market and then the stock market."

Janeway believed that the market would be vulnerable to ups and downs and would not provide the generous rewards it once offered to its investors. He saw Johnson's commitment to providing both guns and butter as a definite mistake; it would, in his view, cause a serious money market crunch. In his newsletter and column he predicted that there would be a soaring federal budget deficit in 1966, accompanied by a squeeze on the money market.

The predictions were based on a logical extrapolation of Johnson's war policy. By refusing to increase taxes to pay for the war machine being constructed by American industry, Johnson was forcing the federal government into heavy borrowing later on in the money market to pay for the expensive hardware and manpower.

This borrowing would cause a surge in the demand for money,

forcing up interest rates. With high interest rates as a primary attraction, both big-investor and small-investor money would be diverted from the stock market into the money market.

Inflation would be the direct result.

In addition to the troubles coming in the American economy, Janeway saw that there would be a plethora of world monetary problems created by the Vietnam War. He predicted that the British pound would be devaluated.

History had already shown that the decline of Great Britain as a world power occurred when the Empire became overextended. Wars growing out of her worldwide commitments had drained her dry. Janeway saw the war in Vietnam as America's colonial war; it too was dislocating and disrupting the functioning of the American economy.

Johnson was wrong, Janeway contended, in pretending that he could handle the war "without having to abandon his dedication to the vision of the Great Society." He was ignoring the first rule of national survival: "that the way to strengthen the sources of military power is to expand the economy."

Janeway even took to the stump to score Johnson's economic policies, especially on an international basis: "The Lyndon Johnson technique of playing consensus politics, which has worked so masterfully in the domestic area, is clearly not working in our monetary negotiations with the European financial powers," he told the New England Bank Management Conference in Boston in the fall of 1965. "The powers that be in European political finance have assumed that Johnson would deal from strength and, accordingly, they have been waiting for America to lead in the move towards modernization of the international monetary mechanism."

But Johnson was not acting. "Instead, to their surprise, Uncle Sam has conned himself into an elaborate Alphonse and Gaston ritual. The spectacle of American leadership seeking to follow nonexistent European agreement, instead of playing upon Europe's readiness to follow the leadership of dollar diplomacy, threatens to put the dollar on the defensive again at the international bargaining table."

All sides, he said, were admitting that the current "antiquated international monetary machinery" was becoming a danger to world stability.

"The $64 question for 1966 is whether American leadership will anticipate and avert the new 1929, of which Federal Reserve Chairman [William McC.] Martin warned last June or whether it will take another 1929 to precipitate modernization of the mechanism."

Harsh words, but something Janeway felt he had to say. Even the pro-Johnson New York *Times* ran the story.

As it turned out, his first predictions were absolutely correct. The stock market took a drubbing in 1966. It reversed the long, steady rise it had enjoyed ever since 1933 and went down—much to the consternation of investors and advisers. In 1967, Britain was forced to devalue the pound, just as Janeway had predicted.

But there was even more bad news in store for the American investor. Although the market reversed its descent and began climbing again in 1966, the budget deficits instituted by the government to pay for the war inflated the currency and caused the dollar to decline.

In 1969 the Federal Reserve Board, panicking over the possibilities of uncontrolled inflation, reversed its easy-money stance and limited the amount of money in circulation. This was a deflationary move, initiated to forestall more inflation. This diverted even more money from the stock market. Because money became more valuable, it could earn greater return elsewhere.

The stock market became even more depressed. For months Janeway warned his readers that the economy was going to suffer both inflation in the economic sector and deflation in the stock market and in profits.

Many of his readers found it difficult to believe him. The two opposite pulling effects had never been linked in the American economy: inflation affected both the economy and the market in the same manner; so did deflation. This contradictory effect was a totally different and unfamiliar response. Janeway was chided by economists for writing contradictory prose.

However, he was right. In 1969 the market was on its way down again after its very long gradual rise from the 1930s.

Since 1951 Janeway had been writing free-lance articles, his column, and his newsletter, and had lectured about the economy. He had also been pondering another book, to be called *The Economics of Crisis: War, Politics, and the Dollar*. It did not appear until 1968, however.

The book was an elaboration of his theory that there was a close relationship between the economy and the waging of war.

"This book attempts to study the economic and financial effects of past crises," he explained in the introduction. "It considers war and wars as the solvent in which economics, finance and politics are dissolved, and out of which new forms, responses and institutions grow.

"We are overdue for a perspective on our economic history which can help to secure our political future; overdue for an economic rationale designed to bring the politics of crisis under control and to finance the prodigious cost it thrusts upon us."

Unlike his earlier books, which dealt with contemporary subjects, *Economics of Crisis* studied war and wars in a historical perspective, comparing the Vietnam debacle with the American Revolution, the Civil War, and World Wars I and II.

Janeway came to the sad conclusion that America's wars had aided our economy: "Does war pay? American idealism has declared that it does not. But American idealism has found itself at odds not only with the Marxist assertion that war pays somebody, if only the 'merchants of death,' but also with American experience. America's wars seem to have paid not only somebody, but usually almost everybody.

"Looking backward over the broad perspective of America's modern economic development, our wars have not been blights, marking social setbacks or disintegration. On the contrary, they stand out as the successive takeoff points in the history of our economic growth and social progress; and, conversely, the successive takeoff points in the history of our economic growth and social progress are marked by wars, or, more specifically, by the economic spillover from successive wars."

In analyzing the outcome of the Civil War, Janeway concluded: "The North won the Civil War in exactly the same way as industrial America has won all her subsequent wars—by the sheer momentum of the war production and the war-supporting production generated behind the lines in her economy."

And, he pointed out, our victory in World War II was achieved the same way. "That magnitude of Roosevelt's gamble on economic momentum to power America's military push may have obscured its family resemblance to the pattern-making strategy Lincoln had adopted eighty years earlier. In fact, Eisenhower laid siege to Europe in the same exasperatingly slow, deadly methodical way in which Grant dug in to take Richmond—and on the same Gargantuan scale."

Both the Civil War and World War II were breaks for America. "America emerged from both the Civil War and World War II with unparalleled opportunities for investment and with a comparably greater store of liquid savings to pump into the investment opportunities which war had opened up.

"From the Civil War to the turn of the century, America grew from the world's leading undeveloped frontier to the threshold of world industrial leadership. . . . Both postwar booms shared another characteristic: they carried domestic dynamism into the international arena. But, whereas the post-Civil-War boom left America poised for successful imperalist adventures in Cuba and the Philippines, the post-World-War-II boom ended by springing an unwanted and treacherous trap in Vietnam. Economic growth, instead of providing the material basis for strategic operations, wound up sacrificed to strategic oversight."

Janeway concluded his book by bringing history up to date with the Vietnam War and its economic consequences: "As the country reacted to . . . the Johnson Administration's failure to develop a plan for financing the war, it discovered that, far from enjoying the best of war and peace, it was suffering the worst of both. . . . As the war grew larger, the economy continued to stagnate and, consequently, its generation of earnings grew smaller. When the emergency burden of financing the cost of government grew relatively larger, and when the Johnson Administration's money-raising requirements accelerated the dangerous process by which the burdens of government eroded the earning power needed to support the government apparatus, the fate of the great post-war bull market in Wall Street was sealed. Thanks to the Vietnam crisis, the first market crash since the coming of the welfare state to America became a clear and present danger."

Janeway was not well received by *The New York Times Book Review*: "One suspects that [this] book will receive short shrift from historians, economists and social scientists alike. Janeway presents a picture of the world, at least of the United States, through glasses so curiously tinted that at times the landscape is almost unrecognizable, and he presents very meager evidence in proportion to the large number of stimulating, occasionally plausible, frequently novel, but probably erroneous propositions.

"Mr. Janeway's view that American economy stagnated in 1967 is hardly borne out by the statistics," the reviewer added, adroitly overlooking the point that Janeway was making: that the economy was in trouble not only at the time he was writing but would be in the future as well. Janeway was right: inflation was in the wings waiting.

What mainly concerned the reviewer was the fact that Janeway's economics didn't seem to fit the pattern of contemporaneous theories and precepts. "One gets the impression from the book, therefore, of a brilliant and insightful mind, untrained in the social sciences, and unaware of the need for the testing of propositions even in history, out of touch with most of the thought in his own field, but nevertheless, because of these very deficiencies, occasionally striking through to very challenging ideas and propositions."

Book World liked Janeway's treatment: "Alongside this analysis," wrote R. J. Whalen, "familiar leftist conceptions about warmaking seem almost childish in their innocence of the realities of power and money. Here we find no sparring with sinister abstract phantoms, such as the proprietors of the 'military-industrial complex,' but, rather, a fascinating account of how scheming, fallible, flesh-and-blood men sought and wielded power in time of crisis."

"An extremely thought-provoking book," said the *Library Journal*.

Best Sellers was negative: "If the reader has the means to follow the meandering facts and events presented in this book, he will learn that the United States has fought a number of wars in its almost two centuries of independence [and that] . . . some of the effects have been favorable, others unfavorable . . . no attempt is made to draw any conclusions from the events or to suggest any development of policies that may be useful in future crises."

Janeway's book helped give him a degree of exposure that his columns and newsletter had not. The news magazines discussed the book, especially the blasts at Johnson, and reviewed his predictions, especially about the possibilities of more inflation in the economy and deflation in the stock market.

His theories began receiving more notice.

In February 1970 Janeway was interviewed at length by *Dun's*

Review. "The problem isn't recession," he said. "It's crash. It's panic.

"The stock market is a death trap right now. In my judgment, January will be the highest month in 1970. Optimistically, I can see the Dow dropping to 625. But if the Fed doesn't turn the monetary situation around in time, I can see a full 50 percent drop from the all-time high. In other words, a 500 Dow."

In May 1970 the Dow Jones average fell from 985.08, reached on November 29, 1968, to 681.08, the biggest decline since the Great Depression—over 300 points in one long slide.

It wasn't a recession that was bothering Janeway: "Before we could ever get to a recession we are going to have a money panic," he said. "It could have been averted yesterday and possibly today. But tomorrow may be too late. The Federal Reserve had been irresponsible and, let's say it, incompetent in pursuing the notion that you can run the economy without liquidity in the banks. What makes it even more outrageous is that the Fed has sanctioned the proliferation of bank credit cards to people who have no need or desire for them, while denying money to businessmen who need short-term loans to meet swollen payrolls. It should slap on credit controls."

Janeway did not mean wage and price controls: "The futile arguments about wage and price controls, which will not work, have obscured the need for credit controls, which will.

"The stock market is not running on its own. It's married to the bond market. And the climate for common stocks will not improve until long-term interest rates come down. But they won't come down unless we get credit controls. If we have credit controls, the Fed will be able to tell the large, capital-intensive corporations to get out of the credit markets and go to their stockholders for money. If this pressure is taken off the money markets, interest rates will come down pretty fast."

When he was asked why the Fed hadn't instituted credit controls, Janeway responded: "Because they're too stupid. They're reading from an obvious textbook and they're being programmed by a computer built to reflect their presumptions. They are also concerned with their credibility gap. Having gone too far in pumping out money in 1965, they are now determined to demonstrate that they mean business even if they have to bring on a financial panic to do it. The Fed has a conflict between its public relations image and a solution to the problem. Their image is apparently given priority by the Board."

In 1970 Janeway produced his first book written to advise the average American investor. Titled *What Shall I Do With My Money?*, it was a how-to-do-it-work showing average men and women how to subsist on their income and get the best value from their money.

In this, an optimistic book, Janeway said that the family budget could be made to cover necessities, recreation, and even include a portion left over for investment.

The stock market was beginning to rise from its 1966 plunge, but as yet it hadn't fully recovered. Nor would it, Janeway told his readers, until there were corrections in the economy that would bring down interest rates. He explained briefly how inflation in the economy and deflation in the stock market could co-exist.

Janeway pointed out that the government had tried to slow down inflation by slowing down the stock market. It had planned its attack on inflation in the mistaken assumption that the market went up when the economy went up, and down when the economy went down. By tampering with the stock market, Janeway noted, Washington thought it could limit inflation. Instead, the result was a depressed stock market and continued inflation.

"For the first time since 1929," he wrote, "investors are confronted by more investment risks than opportunities."

He explained that with an inflated dollar, both business and government were forced to borrow at the same time, competing with each other for the dollars in circulation. "Historically," he pointed out, "in the days before big governments and little wars, there was a rhythm between borrowers and borrowing. When business borrowed, government didn't; when government borrowed, business didn't—as simple as breathing out and breathing in."

Today, he went on, competition between business and government for dollars was driving up interest rates, in turn making it more difficult for both to function. That competition kept interest rates high, depressed business, and depressed the stock market as well—without bringing inflation under control.

The main portions of the book dealt with subjects such as personal finance, harnessing the spending power of cash, real estate, mutual funds, stocks, bonds, and investment advisers. His concluding chapter discussed ways to cope with the overall economy.

Most of the chapters were introduced by general information and then consisted of questions and answers, many of them extracted from Janeway's newsletters and columns. The questions and answers dealt with situations that were both specific and complex. Occasionally Janeway reverted to the one-liners he used in his newsletter:

Q. Would lower interest rates help the stock market?
A. That's like asking me if I could see better if you stopped poking your finger in my eye.

In the final chapter, Janeway discussed three financial rules of thumb that every man and woman should observe:

The first was a political observation: Elect a President who understands finance and its relationship to the economy and who will do something about this relationship.

The second was a financial observation: Wait until long-term investment rates come down before getting back into the stock market or the bond market.

The third was a speculative observation: Wait until the bond market straightens out before investing in the stock market.

When would that be?

After the stock market has had a good long sleep, Janeway wrote. "When it wakes up, it will look back on the last trip it took into get-rich-quick land as an hallucination. The big secret about Wall Street is that while there is a quick way to lose money, there are no quick ways to make it there, nor, indeed anywhere else. Money-making is for those who have saved enough of it to have it to put to work for them."

Janeway's book even described the combined inflation and recession that we have come to know as stagflation.

The reviewer in *The Virginia Quarterly Review* was not totally enraptured by the book or its advice, although he did admit that Janeway understood capital: "[The author] offers sound thinking about the protection of capital. The path laid out toward the goal of capital accumulation, however, is surely nothing less than a banker's fantasy. One begins by laying up from six to nine months' pre-tax income in the savings bank. At the same time, sign up for insurance equivalent to at least five years' worth of pre-tax income. When you can stagger away from this one-two punch you can begin to look around for some mortgaged income-producing property. . . ."

The same reviewer was also bemused by Janeway's answers: "The question and answer sections contain delightful advice," he went on. "My favorite is the suggestion to a man who cannot meet his rent to move into more expensive quarters, for rent hikes are less likely to occur there." The review winds up with: "Highly recommended for widows and orphans."

The *Library Journal* reviewer pointed out that Janeway was "an avowed critic of the Government's economic and financial policies and at this most critical time in our economy he is so disturbed by the prevailing conditions that he has interrupted 'work on a book aimed at guiding Government toward overall solutions to its problems in order to write this one, addressed to the Government's citizens.'"

Two years later, Janeway produced yet another book along the same lines, called *You and Your Money*, billed as an "umbrella against the financial storms still to come."

Although the bulk of it included updated sections resembling those in *What Shall I Do With My Money?*—containing advice on managing personal finances, the value of cash, real estate, mutual funds, stocks, bonds, and investment advisers—*You and Your Money* opened up with several chapters on the ineptitude of the Nixon Administration in dealing with the economy.

The key date, Janeway wrote, was August 15, 1971, the day Nixon imposed price and wage controls and took the dollar off the gold standard, allowing it to float.

"After Nixon successively trusted the old economics to fight recession—and found them both wanting—his imposition of peacetime controls institutionalized a reversal of role. The president, who had been the respectful and acquiescent client, became the playmaker."

Janeway called the situation crisis-ridden at best and elaborated with a typical Janewayism: "The most useful rule of the road for money-users eyeing crisis-time opportunities is summed up in the description of how porcupines make love—'carefully.'"

His recommendation was to give an "overriding priority to cash and putting the burden of proof on arguments for using any of it."

Janeway analyzed the stock market situation in these words: "The story of its own the stock market told in 1971 and 1972 documented its peculiar nature. For the stock market goes with present money conditions, and it anticipates future business conditions. In 1971, money conditions were easy; and business conditions looked good for 1972 'because Nixon has to get reelected.' Moreover, foreign buying was touted as guaranteeing a markup and a bailout to any and all Americans beating it to the sell side of the market. Not until after the market made new highs for volume, but failed to translate them into new highs for the leading averages, did the see-saw tilt the other way. Moreover, just when higher interest rates made money conditions less attractive to investors, lower activity rates made business conditions more uncertain, too—not least thanks to the slump in the overseas economics where the best companies had been recording the most dynamic gains for the most glamorous stocks. Just when the dollar devaluation deal began to come unstuck, the dollar devaluation rally came unstuck with it."

Because of the devaluation fiasco, Janeway's main concern and advice for his readers was to conserve cash in the coming years, until the economy straightened out. He also advised his readers to maintain savings at a high level and to buy assets and securities only when they offered investment values on a bargain basis.

The stock market had lost its image as a symbol of prosperity and a hedge against inflation. "The money-using people in this country not only have dollars, they have sense," he wrote in his usual tongue-in-cheek fashion. "Having once decided that the stock market was more for gamblers than investors, they concluded that the turf there was too fast for them, and the payback there both too skimpy and too risky.

"The flight of amateur investors from the high risks and low returns offered by the stock market has raised the risk and lowered the return on staying in it."

He predicted that the amateurs would return, not to the glamour issues, but to the workhorse "income" stocks, whose payoffs would be up. Oil stocks, perhaps. Utility stocks when the price was right.

Mutual funds presented another problem: "The most relevant fact to bear in mind is that the mutual funds with the best and most consistent performance records were created before and during the depression, and have enjoyed a consistent rise since.

. . . [However] . . . few mutual funds which have outperformed the pack in any given year have ever managed to put anything like three outstanding years back to back." And: "The rule for mutual funds is that consistency of good performance is bought at the price of spectacular but erratic performance. The impressive growth of the mutual fund industry has brought with it a tendency to exaggerate its importance."

As for the bond market, he repeated that a fall in interest rates and a rise in bond prices would be a reliable leading indicator of a follow-through rise in stock prices. In other words, the future of the stock market and the bond market lay in the actions of interest rates.

Janeway concluded with a reminder: "Market moves result from the continuing interplay of at least three interacting factors. Actual changes in money conditions are the first. Expected changes in business conditions are the second. Changes in political bets are the third."

"Another look at the state of our economy," A. J. Anderson wrote for the *Library Journal*, "and in many ways one of the most helpful we have had so far. The author . . . tells what he thinks is wrong with the economy (he announces that Nixon's new economic program has failed), and suggests ways that the government might extricate itself from its money troubles. . . . Janeway's book also offers a short, solid course on managing one's personal finances, with advice on handling mutual funds, property, stocks, bonds, and cash."

Four years later Janeway wrote *Musings on Money: How to Make Dollars Out of Sense*. This book contained not specific advice for making money, but more general opinions. For example:

"Your feelings about money reflect your feelings about yourself."

"We've paid a lot of taxes, but how much civilization have we received in return?"

"Living with the stock market is a lot like having a marriage that runs into problems, but works."

And he took potshots at politicians:

"When Nixon bulled the price of gold, he confirmed the lesson of the early Roosevelt years: A higher price of gold contributes to more inflation, not less.

"He chose the right time to do the wrong thing: unleashing more inflation as an antidote to too much inflation."

Although the treatment was interesting and the text easily readable, the "musings" were just about exactly that—random observations on things economic and financial, including anecdotes of his early days.

"Many people may call this a book," *Best Sellers* wrote. "It is actually a collection of paragraphs. The paragraphs are supposed to be the distilled wisdom of a many years of experience on Wall Street. Many of them are nothing more than plain common sense, some are trite old sayings."

Library Journal recognized that Janeway's reputation was enough to make the book important, if the content did not: "In general, the work is somewhat disjointed and short on substance, but the Janeway name makes it a necessary purchase nonetheless."

Janeway never confined himself to predictions in his column and in his newsletter, or in his books. For some years now he had been holding annual meetings in Washington, employing well-known and respected figures in economics and finance to appear in a kind of round-robin panel arrangement to speak before a paying audience.

In the years since 1966, when his first pronouncements on the shakiness of the economy were made, he had become recognized as a male Cassandra who saw only trouble in the years ahead, and by 1979 he was known as "Calamity Janeway."

Janeway was not alone in his negative readings of the stock

market and of the economy in general. Other prognosticators, particularly competitors in the financial newsletter business, were underlining his negativism, some of them calling it their own, and rarely admitting that Janeway had seen it all before them.

The success of Janeway's Washington Seminars, as he called them, was said to be due more to his sense of showmanship and drama than to the words uttered by the participants. As master of ceremonies, Janeway usually ran his show while seated in the audience like a friendly upfront stage manager, jumping up to ask a question or interrupting a question and answer session with elucidations and disputations.

Naturally, one of the purposes of the seminars was to promote his newsletters and spread the word about his column. Quotations from the platform frequently made the newspapers or provoked comment on television shows about finance.

For his 1979 seminar, Janeway invited Senator Howard Baker of Tennessee; Governor Bob Ray of Iowa; Dr. Tom Nesbitt, president of the American Medical Association; Al Sindlinger, an economic and political pollster; and William Tehan, a gold analyst with P. R. Herzig & Company.

A great deal of political discussion ensued between Janeway and Baker and Ray, but when Sindlinger got on the stage, the subject turned to inflation. Janeway sparred with him in typical fashion.

"Our key problem," said Sindlinger at one point, "is that we're running the nation on the belief that our inflation rate is someplace around 18 percent. This is a gross fallacy."

Up popped Janeway. "Al, my dear friend, the good doctor, said 9 percent. How far out of it can you be?"

"What good doctor?"

"Doctor Tom Nesbitt, this morning."

"That the inflation rate is 9 percent?"

"You know what he's doing. He doesn't play this game. All

he's doing is parroting the official idiocy." Janeway meant the Administration pronouncements of President Jimmy Carter.

"That is correct," Al Sindlinger agreed. "We are anticipating—and if you would stop and listen to my poll interviews of these idiots who are buying stock right now because they are convinced that the recession is going to bring down inflation, and that the stock market is about ready to take off—these idiots believe that rising interest rates are going to control the inflation problem."

"Excuse me again," Janeway interrupted. "They also believe that rising interest rates are going to depress gold prices. But rising interest rates will really continue to *inflate* gold prices."

"That is correct. When I talked to you last year when the official government inflation rate was 8 percent, I was saying it was really 10 percent. My data says that the inflation rate at the present time is 18 percent and by the end of the year it will be 20 percent or 21."

Janeway: "Interrupt again. Al, the two price indices are indices of prices of goods, is that right?"

"That's right. And *I'm* talking about the prices that people pay to live."

"Right. But, Al, inflation has all along been paced not by the price of an automobile or a sink, but the cost of repairing, is that right?"

"Right."

"So the repairs are not in the index, right?"

"That's right."

"So pragmatically, rule of thumb, if the official number is an admitted 14 percent, therefore, being generous, if you allow just a 3 percent override as a repair cost, while the service costs generally—taxes, insurance premiums, interest, whatever—you're up to 18 percent."

"Now, you are under the impression, if you listen to those interviews with people who are buying stocks, that the Federal

Reserve Board is creating tight money," Sindlinger went on. "We don't have tight money. The Federal Reserve Board *isn't* controlling interest rates. Mr. Volcker is doing what he has to do, and that is to keep money from becoming cheaper each week than it was the week before. Because you've got to have, to keep any economy functioning, an interest rate that is at least 2 percent and possibly 3 percent above the inflation rate. Therefore, if the inflation rate is now 18 percent, which I say it is, you're going to have the discount rate at 20 percent and you're going to have a prime interest rate at 22 percent!"

Janeway agreed: "The most profitable investment the average man can make in this country today," he went on, "is to fight the consumerists in his or her community, borrow anything at any rate, and buy an apartment."

Later, in an interview with the gold analyst William Tehan, Janeway gave his views on the rise in gold prices: "If gold goes up this way to 500," he said, "you've got to figure, I promise you, that tops for gold, or the rate of climb, is not being dictated by market factors but by the length of time it will take for the United States to get out of this political vacuum. And we can't do it until January 1981.

"South Africa has the world's largest uranium-export capabilities. And I believe that in 1981 or 1982 their gold-mine stocks will be investment values primarily for their uranium production with their gold flows being usable as by-products. If I am right, and I don't see how I can miss, in view of what's going on in the nuclear power race, I think we're looking at $80 uranium. This is the only investment-for-income strategy that defends you against the numbers Sindlinger has been projecting."

What actually happened with gold, of course, was an unprecedented and shattering rise to $875 in the first months of 1980, after which came a shuddering drop back into the trough, eventually to bottom out in the low $300s. Uranium stocks never approached the predicted highs.

One reporter complimented Janeway on the entertainment value of his seminar. Janeway sighed with disappointment. "Well, you see, that's the story of my life. That's the word that came to your lips—'entertaining.' A lot of people think that because I make it entertaining it ain't thunderingly and thunderously serious."

In spite of Janeway's coy protestations about the effectiveness of his roving commentator approach, he was gaining more public support in his somewhat counterestablishment ideas about the economy and the stock market.

Early in 1980 Janeway agreed to be interviewed by one of the editors of *Forbes*. "I erred in talking to these people," he wrote later. As a result of the meeting, in its March 31 issue, *Forbes* published a profile of Janeway titled, "Right Yes, Omniscient No."

Forbes not only interviewed him but read back through two years of his newsletter, by then known as *The Janeway Letter*, and reported him to have been overly optimistic about General Public Utilities and Chrysler, and overly pessimistic about oil company stocks in January 1979, advising his readers to sell "just before they took off."

The magazine pointed out, however, that he had advised in late 1977 to sell U.S. stocks and buy South African gold issues, and that he had predicted the crash in the bond market, with its outrageously high short-term interest rates.

Janeway was quoted as saying, "The price of oil is going to crash." He was said to be "gloomy" about the U.S. economy "more so than ever, it seems." And he was reported to be touting South African gold stocks, reasoning that gold and the U.S. stock market move in opposite directions.

Forbes was unhappy about Janeway's optimism over Chrysler. In July Janeway called it "the most explosive breakaway stock on the [big] Board." Chrysler was $10 at that time, *Forbes* pointed out; in March 1980, at the time of the *Forbes* article, it was $9. Its future, *Forbes* wrote, was "uncertain."

The profile wasn't totally negative, but it did underline Janeway's new image as one of the doom-and-gloom prognosticators.

Janeway's reaction was predictable. He immediatcly wrote a long letter correcting certain assertions in *Forbes* that he felt were incorrect. *Forbes* printed some of the comments, but not the letter in toto. Janeway immediately spent $7,000 on advertisements, publishing his entire letter of rebuttal.

In an advertisement headlined "A Message from Eliot Janeway," which ran in several publications, among them *Barron's*, he confronted his critics.

He cited examples in which he was not "persistently" prone to "doom-and-gloom pronouncements." He had been optimistic, he said, when in 1963 he predicted that the Dow would top 1000 within a year. Actually, it took thirteen months. He pointed out that in 1974 he told his readers to switch out of gold stocks and go back into U.S. securities. He also pinpointed the utilities as the leaders of the 1974 recovery. They led it.

He mentioned that his supposed "optimism about General Public Utilities" was created in *Forbes'* mind because he had branded the meltdown scare during the hysteria over the Three Mile Island plant failure as phony. However, in 1977, he had recommended selling all utility stocks. Was that optimism?

He also objected to this statement: "He missed the silver boom and advised selling the international oil stocks before they took off." Janeway's comment: What boom? What takeoff?

Finally, Janeway disputed *Forbes'* contention that "Janeway is still gloomy about the American economy." But Janeway protested that all his magazine and newspaper ads had said in plain English: "No U.S. recession,—just a disaster in Wall Street!"

Janeway wrote: "If we are suffering from a recession, it will be the first on record in which travelers with unlimited expense accounts can't find a hotel room! If the economy is driven to the dogs by Carter's quackery, its trouble will become plain enough to show that the argument about a mere recession has all along been academic. The danger then would be a full-fledged depression, not just a recession."

He ended his advertisement by saying: "Certainly, it is true that no one is infallible; but some financial writers are more inaccurate than others, and some financial editors are more irresponsible than others in their errors of omission."

He concluded with the following valedictory: "Yours for smuggling ethics into journalism."

What does Eliot Janeway's track record look like? Actually, quite good.

• In 1965 he predicted that the stock market would take a drubbing in 1966. He was right. It made its first big postwar drop to 774.88.

• In 1966 he predicted that Britain would devalue the pound. He was right; it was devalued in 1967.

• In 1969 he said that America would suffer a combination of inflation in the economy and deflation in the stock market. He was right; the brand-new syndrome was called stagflation.

• In 1970 he predicted that the stock market would drop to a low of 625; it was 985 at the time. He was almost right. In May 1970 the market declined over 350 points to 631.16.

• In 1974 he forecast that the Dow Jones would approach 450 that year. It didn't hit 450, but it did bottom out at 577.60. When Janeway made his prediction, on January 1, the Dow stood at 850.

• In 1975 and 1976 Janeway insisted that the economy was sick, despite statistics that showed growth. He was wrong. The economy was healthy and did show recovery. The stock market turned bullish.

- In 1975 through 1978, he paid no attention to the bull market in American Stock Exchange and over-the-counter issues, which reached new highs in 1978. He picked up on them then, but warned: "Junk stocks never start bull market recoveries."

- In July 1975 he said that the price of gold, then at $170 an ounce, would fall back to $100. It went down to $103 in 1976.

- In 1977 he predicted that interest rates would be "significantly lower" than in the spring. They did not go down.

- In 1978 he predicted that in 1979 there would be a severe slump plus runaway inflation, marked by record-high interest rates. He was right.

- In 1978 he said gold would make a "slow but sure" climb during the second half of the year. He was right.

- In 1979 he predicted a high for the Dow of around 880 or 890. It hit 897.61 on October 5.

- In 1979 he changed his prediction of a "slow but sure" climb for gold into a strong bull market. The price of gold reached $875 in 1980. It did retreat, of course, down to $530 soon afterward.

- In 1979 he predicted the bubble and bust for silver. (Janeway did not predict a boom, as *Forbes* wrote; hence his correction in his advertisement.) Silver rose from $1.60 an ounce to $48 in 1979–1980. Had it remained at $48, Janeway would have conceded it to have been a boom. It immediately fell once again, almost to its former level—a bust.

- Janeway had been predicting high interest rates all along, ever since 1977, when he had mistakenly called for them to go down. He was right in the long run: they continued on their way up.

- He predicted the end of Detroit's domination of the world car market. He predicted the boom in auto imports. He was right on both counts.

• He correctly predicted the continued markup in property values, all through the 1970s and 1980s.

• He called Chrysler "a once-in-a-lifetime special situation" in 1979. In the middle of 1982, Chrysler was suddenly in the black; its preferred stock stood in the low $20s in the spring of 1983. He could turn out to be right in the long run.

Where do we go from here?

"Inflation is going to be roaring, raging, rampaging, hyped up," Janeway said in a 1981 interview in *50 Plus*, a magazine for persons over fifty. "For at least the first half of the 1980s it's going to run to 20 percent or more a year, no matter what the official figures might say."

What does he advise for those men and women who are being "swindled by inflation" and a government that can't bring it down?

"You need stretchable assets that will produce 20 to 50 percent more income every year. Some selective real estate can produce. But real estate calls for management, capital, experience, and ingenuity. Real estate isn't for many people."

Where can you find stretchable assets?

"In gold mining stocks. I expect the Dow Jones Industrial Average to go down as low as 600 after it hits a high-volume trading figure of seventy to eighty million shares for several days. Then it will be swamped with sellers and collapse to that 600 range. But even when the Dow falls, most of the gold mining stocks—South African, not American—will do well."

Most of all, Janeway's advice seems to be: "Get capital, no matter where you are, get capital."

2
Joseph Granville

Almost a thousand of the faithful had assembled at Caesars Atlantic City casino to greet their self-appointed leader. They were a typical cross-section of Americans anxious to do their best in the battle against inflation. They wanted investment advice for the stock market—and the man they had come to see provided that advice for them.

Although many had come to enjoy a little gambling at the Atlantic City tables, they were not high-rolling as they waited for the arrival of their mentor. Suddenly there was a hushed silence as the double doors opened and two well-dressed young men appeared, wheeling in an open coffin containing a tall, lanky man stretched out under a shroud of ticker tape. Dressed in a suit, with a martini in one hand and a cigarette in the other, Joseph Granville lay there solemnly with his eyes closed and trying to suppress a smile.

Now the loudspeaker blared Granville's theme song, the words to which had been solemnized by many a stock market investor as "Darling, they're playing our song."

In part, the song went:

> Winners and losers, gamblers and boozers,
> If they zig every time they should zag
> They're following the news, the obvious views
> And they're caught, baby, holding the bag.

Written by Granville himself, the song was titled "The

Bagholder Blues." In his personalized vocabulary, a "bagholder" was a banker, an investment broker, or an investor who did not buy low and sell high—in other words, an innocent who was left holding the bag.

Those of the faithful huddled near the coffin saw Granville open his eyes and make a move to sit up. But one young associate hissed out in a stage whisper: "Stay in there until I tell you!"

The song ran its course. Finally it was time for the resurrection, and Granville sat up stiffly, taking a slug of his martini.

"I'm rising from the dead!" he screamed loudly into a microphone that had appeared at his mouth as if by magic. "Now, boys, get me out of this goddamned thing!"

The messiah's followers roared their approval, bursting into applause. It was a typical opening for a Granville show. Many of those present had been to one or more prior to this one. Others had seen him on national television propounding his views on the stock market. Still others had read, studied, and perhaps memorized his book, A *Strategy of Daily Stock Market Timing for Maximum Profit,* a handbook he had written many years before and which had proved itself by its endurance and effectiveness, particularly for the small investor.

The "resurrection" theme was typically Granvillean show-biz hype. Four months earlier, in January 1981, he had flashed a sell signal to the subscribers of his popular newsletter. With the market at 1004.69, hundreds of his followers had bailed out, triggering a one-day panic on Wall Street.

With thousands of investors unloading their holdings simultaneously, trading on the New York Stock Exchange hit a record 93,000,000 shares. The Dow Jones tumbled 24 points. Granville had enhanced his image as a technical forecaster, but insiders claimed that they and other forecasters had warned of minor adjustments that would be made in the market; Granville, they said, had simply used his knowledge of these difficulties to precipitate a fall that would make him seem capable of precognition.

However, the fact that Granville was right—or, as others would have it, that his advice had caused a slide—boomeranged on him. He had said that stock prices would fall "straight down," and they did. During that day, many of his newsletter subscribers had desperately tried to sell before their stocks fell below purchase price. Many of them didn't get out in time and lost money in the slide.

In addition, the news services had picked up Granville's predictions and had passed them on to the public. This meant that many non-Granvilleites were able to unload, taking advantage of his warning. Thus, many of Granville's faithful lost money.

There was one more wrinkle, typical of Granville's service, that militated against his faithful followers. His newsletter cost $250 a year, but for $500 extra he had also instituted a special "early-warning service" by telephone to apprise subscribers of sudden rallies or dips.

Those who paid only $250 for the newsletter didn't receive the telephoned advice and were not in on the sell everything signal he sent out on January 6. They were caught in the downslide and lost heavily, like thousands of others who tried to unload.

Those who hung on—non-Granvilleites—made out better than the faithful. Although the market kept tumbling the second day—adding another 15 points—it recovered on Friday and settled in at 968.69 by the end of the week, only 30-odd points off its previous high. By April 27, it was at 1024.05.

Of Granville's subscribers, 1,300 decided that they had been taken for a ride and canceled. And Granville made one other slight miscalculation. He had begun to dabble in seismology, and had come up with the astonishing prediction that on April 10 the entire West coast would slide off into the Pacific in a monstrous quake, more than 8 on the Richter Scale.

Nothing happened—not even a tremor. The believers were somewhat shaken by God's apparent desertion of Granville. The prophet was unavailable for comment. A spokesman said: "He's a great market forecaster but not much of a seismologist."

Granville, the seer, in effect, had died twice, and the show at Caesars was his resurrection.

After finishing his martini and cigarette, Granville went into his act, a somewhat chastened man. A tall, craggy, hawkish, hungry-looking, bug-eyed twentieth-century Barnum, he was all show-business after his opening remarks.

He said he was going to do less clowning and more teaching. He had made a mistake in not warning his subscribers ahead of time in January; he apologized for putting them in a bind in which they couldn't unload their stocks before the prices tumbled. He blamed their dilemma on the fact that the news services had broadcast his advice worldwide.

But nothing could keep the ebullient Granville down. "I've become a one-man market indicator," he told them. "Probably the only live one you've ever seen on an American stage." And he said the Dow would drop as much as 400 points in "the great bear market of 1981–1982."

But he was very bullish about the future of the stock market.

"The gaming stocks were lemons last year in the face of a 245-point rise in the market. It's equally logical that they'll rise in a huge decline."

Reactions to Granville's resurrection proved mixed: "I thought he was drunk," one of his followers confided. "It's just a disgrace compared with shows he's put on before."

Granville's reaction? "Sure, I was a little looser than normal, but sometimes you have to fall down on the stage to wake people up."

Joseph Ensign Granville was born in Yonkers, New York, in 1923. His father was a banker who had begun the long upward struggle to respectability as a runner on Wall Street, working his way painfully through the banking structure, to lose everything in the 1929 Stock Market Crash.

"It wasn't the market that did it," Granville once maintained. "It was Wall Street." Then, on a more confident note: "If he had followed what I teach now, he'd have made $8,000,000 on the Crash!" Unluckily, Granville wasn't then the oracle that he later proclaimed himself to be. Nor was he then old enough to provide his father with any advice.

Granville's mother came from a well-to-do family, had been a debutante, and was a lifelong believer in the occult, including its modern manifestation, extrasensory perception. When he was sixteen, she sent Granville to the world-famous psychic Edgar Cayce for a life reading. What that reading said is not known. Even Cayce couldn't have predicted all the ups and downs that were going to affect the young Yonkers prodigy.

For a prodigy he was. With his quick mind, high IQ, and swift perceptions, he was too intellectually developed for his slower classmates. The family borrowed enough money to send him to Todd, a private school in Woodstock, Illinois. It was known as an institution for gifted young men; Orson Welles studied there before he appeared on Broadway.

It was at Todd that Granville began dabbling in one of his primary interests—writing. He published his first full-length book, *A Schoolboy's Faith*. It contained a quatrain of blank verse that was self-revealing:

Bless yourself, Joseph Granville.
Next to God you know yourself
Better than any other mortal
Your ego craves to be understood intelligently.

He was absolutely right. Although the term "ego trip" had not yet been invented, it would accurately describe many of his later ventures into showmanship, dramaturgy, and messianism.

After graduation from Todd, Granville didn't bother entering college. First, his family had no money to send him to the "right" school, even if he had been accepted. And Granville had little

interest in or patience with the classic strictures of learning, evaluating, and thinking. For him the future held other possibilities.

In the Midwest there was a traveling theatrical company called
the Valdes Players. Granville tried out with them, won a place
for himself, and played a number of roles, including ones by
Ibsen and Coward. Flamboyant, loud, and magnetic, he was a
good performer.

"I was born a ham," he said. "I always had the lead in every
school play. I was always the prince." (He was referring to a role
he had played in the fourth grade in Yonkers in a Christmas
version of the *Nutcracker Suite.*)

With the money he had made treading the boards for Valdes,
Granville enrolled at Duke University. J. B. Rhine had made the
university famous for the course in parapsychology he was pio-
neering there. Granville's encounter with Edgar Cayce as a
youth, and the obvious interest of his mother in the "other
world," combined to guide him into the study of parapsychology.

Once enrolled, however, he soon tired of it. He believed that
its obsession with scientific procedure and the rigorous records
demanded of the experiments detracted from any excitement and
interest he might have felt in the subject of extrasensory perception. Besides, he felt that being in parapsychology set him apart
on campus as some kind of freak.

If he were going to set his mind on a course in scientific
method, in the rigors of mathematics, he decided, he would do it
in a more traditional way. He switched his major to chemistry
and found its clear-cut cause and effect rules relaxing and "safe"
after his brief flirtation with the occult. Even so, the mixing of
hydrogen and oxygen to get water wasn't really Granville's idea of
a grand design of life. Chemistry, for all its challenges to the
intellect, wasn't flamboyant enough for his dramatic urges.

He switched to a pre-med course. The image of the doctor
appealed to him. It was now 1943, and the country was at war.
With parapsychology a thing of the past, and with chemistry only

a part of his field of study, Granville realized that he could easily become a doctor if only he could complete his studies under the auspices of Uncle Sam.

In 1945 two momentous events occured in Granville's life. He fell in love with a young graduate named Katherine Reese and married her. And he completed the first two years of his training under the Armed Services College Degree program. He was required to join one of the armed services and opted for the Navy.

The war in the Pacific was going full tilt while the war in Europe was reaching its tumultuous climax. Granville was sent to the tiny atoll of Roy Namur in the Marshall Islands in the remote South Pacific. He found the routine there to be deadly dull. His restless mind took up another challenge. Granville had been interested in collecting stamps from the time he was six years old. He had brought a Scott Catalogue with him and now decided to utilize known technical principles of statistical extrapolation and monetary trends to find out the current worth of all the United States commemorative stamps listed in the catalogue.

He made his predictions in the form of two book-length monographs. He had collected stamps as a child; he had always been interested in the occult, especially in its ability to predict the future; he had dabbled in the hard sciences and knew scientific discipline; he had come by his interest in money honestly through his banker father. It was not really at all strange for him to combine many of his previous interests and talents to come up with a prediction of stamp prices.

"It was through reading my mother's astrology magazines that I first became interested in time cycles," he said. Time cycles had an obvious affinity with price trends. "That was the precursor of my stock market theories," he recalled.

After being mustered out of the Navy at the close of the war, Granville returned to civilian life as a student at Duke, where he finished up his two years of study to graduate; by now he had switched to economics. His earlier forays into hard science and pre-medicine had encouraged him to conquer the field of economics, where both money and prediction played a decisive role. There was the excitement of gambling to pique his interest, along with the precision of mathematics and financial dynamics.

His return to married life did not meet with success. "When I came back from the war we were strangers," he said of himself and his wife, Katherine. "One night I awakened in a cold sweat and said, 'Honey, we're splitting.'"

He never saw her again.

After winding up his studies at Duke, he moved back to New York, the money capital of the country, besides being his hometown, and took graduate work in economics at Columbia University. He was determined by now to concentrate on this interesting and rewarding field.

In order to make ends meet he returned to his early interest in philately. He published a newsletter on stamp collecting, discussing trends in certain types of investments in stamps, which are only now becoming recognized as one of the most lucrative of the collectibles.

He fell in love again. In 1949 he married Pauline Delp, a pianist who had been trained at Juilliard. They settled in New Jersey. The Granvilles began a family, which increased through the years until there were eight children. His newsletter didn't bring in enough money to support his growing household, and he was forced into various lines of employment, but nothing really jelled for him. Economics had not given him, as he had hoped, a magical entrée into the big-money job on Wall Street.

In spite of constant rebuffs, he continued to set up interviews with prospective investment firms. He was interviewed by Merrill Lynch; they were interested. However, when he took the aptitude test he scored in such a way that the company had second thoughts about hiring him. His profile showed that he had absolutely no natural talent for the stock market. He was rejected.

Still Granville persisted. He went to E. F. Hutton. The company was only mildly interested in him until he began talking about the two books he had written on the trend of stamp prices. Hutton needed a competent writer to handle their market letter. They asked to see his books.

That did it. They were impressed by his ability to make the dull price-commentary come to life, and the books showed that he had a flair for predicting monetary trends. They hired him to edit their newsletter. He joined E. F. Hutton in October 1957.

"I was launched the same day as Sputnik."

Writing a daily market letter for E. F. Hutton proved to be more of a problem for them than for Joe Granville. Although his technical market analyses were quite within the limits of Wall Street methodology, his inferential assumptions were sometimes hard for the staid market types to take.

Although the field of market forecasting was pretty well established in the 1950s, many investment firms considered it about on a par with gazing into a crystall ball. "I was a freak," Granville said. "I was somebody who read the entrails in his coffee cup. I was a guru. I was a magician. That was how technicians were viewed in those days. People who looked at the hen scratchings on a piece of paper and read the market."

Granville was not a freak, he was an iconoclast. He broke with almost all the theories beloved by his superiors. "Granville was entirely self-taught," one of his co-workers at Hutton said. "He never gave the impression that he was learning anything from anybody."

He had daily run-ins with hostile fundamental analysts, those who studied the companies, their management, their expertise, and their dividends and earnings rather than the stock market and its movements exclusively.

James Dines, who made his own name later on as a market analyst, recalled those times: "When we arrived on the Street in the 1950s, young analysts were not encouraged to use technical

analysis. You really had to pretend that you didn't use charts—
technical analysis was left to the mavericks."

"Joe was his own man," recalled Robert Stovall, his boss at
Hutton. "Even then he attracted acolytes. The type of guy who
wears an overcoat in the summer would hang around him and
discuss silver or the planets."

He had a certain charisma. Called a "delightful weirdo" by
one of his associates, he was soon known as "Dr. Goebbels" after
the minister of propaganda who whipped the German masses
into action for Hitler. He had, according to another, a "gaunt,
driven look, with bulging eyes and a throbbing Adam's apple."

"A very likable guy," said one colleague. "You could even
make fun of him and he wouldn't mind at all."

With his need to put something down on paper every working
day, Granville found it difficult to remain complaisant and
stodgy. His remarks sometimes became tendentious, then outright presumptuous. He began to make some rather wild predictions, whereas his job should have been confined to veiled
assertions or vague references.

After he had been at Hutton only a few months, he issued a
letter titled "Are the Russians in the U.S. Market?" This piece of
imaginative journalism contained the following scenario, a chain
of ifs: If the Russians, unknown to anyone, managed to invest
over 3 to 5 percent of their enormous defense budget in the U.S.
stock market through blind buyers; if they managed to systemati-
cally accumulate a number of shares of the leading thirty industrials on the Dow Jones list; if they suddenly pressed a button and
sold every one of their shares; if the sudden sales precipitated a
crisis on Wall Street, sending the market down with no chance to
rally; if the fall created another 1929 type of tailspin; if such
happened, the U.S. economy might collapse. *If, if, if . . .*

Even in 1957 Granville was showing his knowledge of the
inner workings of the stock market—the kind of knowledge he
would later exploit in 1981 when he ordered his followers to sell,
sell, sell, and precipitated his own wipeout.

The Russian scenario appealed to Walter Winchell, who was still grinding out a daily gossip column and always needed sensational anti-communist material. He ran a piece on the Granville article, scaring the wits out of half of his readers. It was strictly a tale made out of smoke, but the government bought it, too.

None other than the Central Intelligence Agency began prowling around trying to find out who Joe Granville was. Their investigation was short-lived, but it bothered E. F. Hutton.

Granville was not fired. His copy was simply looked at with a great deal more attention than it had been previously. Not only was it gazed at and second-guessed before it even went out in the form of the daily letter, but it was changed upstairs.

At first the changes were minor.

But then Granville appeared on the Mike Wallace television show. That was in 1961, when he had become fairly well ensconced at Hutton. Wallace was running one of the first of the soon-to-be-immensely popular talk shows. His show had an edge to it—he could come at his interviewees with a scalpel; he throve on controversy and the amazing statement.

Granville was perfect in the role. When Wallace began questioning him about some of the currently popular stocks, Granville came out with a blockbuster: Standard Oil of New Jersey —then trading in the 70s—would soon fall to the 40s.

Mike Wallace didn't operate in a vacuum. Within hours there were complaints being formulated against Hutton. Letters began to flow in, even some telegrams. There was a hasty meeting upstairs. Granville was not to be fired, but he was to be . . . *watched*.

What had been insignificant editorial changes in his daily copy now became big ones. At first Granville put on the best face he could, although he continued to complain that he was being fettered. His family obligations were growing and the bills never stopped coming in. He champed at the bit, but he continued to pull the cart by minding his p's and q's at E. F. Hutton.

On his own time Granville wrote a book about stock market analysis. Called by the rather awkward title A *Strategy of Daily Stock Market Timing for Maximum Profit*, it was published in 1960 by Prentice Hall and included a minute point-by-point method of analyzing stock market trends. It was an instant hit on Wall Street.

"When I got into the business twenty years ago, Joe's book was probably the first thing I read on the subject of technical analysis that excited me enough to pursue it as a career," one now highly-respected technician remembered.

Although considered a non-book by the reviewers, it was a readable and understandable exercise in complicated market analysis. Granville divided it into four basic parts:

- Day-to-day stock market indicators;

- Intermediate stock market indicators;

- Long-range stock market indicators;

- The grand strategy of stock trading.

In his preface, he explained the threefold purpose of the book:
(1) To show the user what to look for in the market;
(2) To interpret the information once identified;
(3) To act on that interpretation in the most profitable manner.

The first three sections were strictly analytical guides. The fourth (numbered V because the introduction was numbered I) was the "grand strategy" of trading. At the beginning of each section he started off with a legend: "Here You Will Learn . . ."

The section on day-to-day market indicators included fifty-five basic indicators, each one a combination of several smaller indicators, or signs easily read in stock market reports, such as market averages, most-active-stocks volume, new highs and lows, and the Dow Jones Industrial Average.

The first of the fifty-five is typical: "(1) When the number of declines outnumbers advances together with a rise in the Dow Jones Industrial Average, then the market is on the verge of a decline."

Later he used two pages to explain by example just what that "indicator" message meant and how it worked to unlock the secret movement of the market.

In each of the fifty-five cases, he explained the indicator and then gave examples.

In the second section (Section III because of the introduction) he covered what he called Intermediate Term Indicators, starting out with the Confidence Indicator and including others such as the Advance-Decline Line and the Six-Month Capital Gain Indicator. These were in turn explained, analyzed, and illustrated with examples from the market.

In the third section he covered other concepts outside the market that might have an effect on it—such as the Wholesale-Retail Concept, Working in a Bull Market, Working in a Bear Market, and the London Market.

In the section on the grand strategy of stock trading, he included instructions on chart reading, an analysis of chart patterns, technical inspection, and other concepts such as the five-minute quiz before buying a stock.

The book, printed on large 8" by 11" pages, was almost 300 pages long—an indication of the amount of material contained in it. The paragraphs were long, but simply written, with Granville-type subheads breaking up the type area. Typical of his sense of humor and casual attitude were one-liners such as:

"Every little movement has a meaning of its own."
"If it's obvious to the public it's obviously wrong."
"Develop a green thumb for stocks."
"Like an amateur boxer, the market telegraphs its punches."
"If you can't beat it—join it."

On page 9 he elucidated his theory of the importance of technical analysis over fundamental analysis when he wrote: "Probably what prompted the writing of this book more than any other single thing is that so often misspent efforts go into the determination of a stock's value—(e.g., earnings, dividends, management changes, etc.) and these efforts often go up in smoke because no effort was made to assess the *timing* of the market. ONLY SUPPLY AND DEMAND MOVES STOCK PRICES and that is measured in terms of money moving into stocks and out of stocks and it is this movement that is first detected by the *technical market indicators*. In short, fundamental stock analysis is of very minor value in terms of timing the market."

The book was still in print in the 1970s, after fifteen-odd printings and soon became a Bible of the technical stock market analyst profession.

It was in 1961 that Granville developed what he later called his On Balance Volume Indicator, or OBV. "I was sitting on the toilet," he recalled with typical Granvillean calculated tastelessness, "staring at the pattern of hexagonal tiles on the floor—those little tiles are a great catalyst of creative thinking." Price, he reasoned, was merely a form of supply and demand; supply and demand were reflected in the *volume* of transactions.

At the time, technicians used the traditional advance/decline indicator based on the price itself. Granville decided to switch to an indicator based on changes in volume, which should precede movements in price. It was a brilliant insight, an elegantly simple idea.

He explained his system in terms understandable to a person not involved in the day-to-day moves of the stock market. "When you throw a ball into the air, it has upward momentum. Before the ball drops, the upward momentum drops sharply. The ball is still rising, but the upward momentum is falling. You know that it will reach its top soon. In the same way, when the majority of my indicators signal a new bottom or top, I know to flash the buy or sell signal."

The "indicators" Granville referred to were of course the ones about which he had written in his book—day-to-day indicators, intermediate indicators, and others used by analysts from the days of C. H. Dow.

He began working on his new indicator, trying to meld it with more traditional ones. He traced its efficacy through market readings and decided it was a solid idea.

"It was a breakthrough that future generations of technicians will look back on," James Dines commented. But not all brokers were as enamoured of it as Dines and the technicians. Said one: "It's the live fish that swims against the stream, not dead ones that float along with it. The approach is meaningless."

Meanwhile, back at the office and out of the men's room, the anti-Granville forces at E. F. Hutton were growing more clamorous.

The brass assigned him a "partner" to help him with his copy. The partner did most of the blue-penciling, on orders from above.

"Nobody blue-pencils me," Granville said indignantly. He began to look for a way out. Meanwhile, the blue pencil was doing more and more damage each day to his prose. He made mild protests at first, and then louder ones, in his typical exaggerated style. The Hutton hierarchy was disinclined to make the outright decision to fire him; too many readers of the newsletter liked his way with words and ideas.

But things were coming to a boil. The blue-penciling and tightening of the fetters finally disenchanted Granville completely. He had put aside a little money from the profits of his book, and had made money on the stamp newsletter. He wanted to try the effectiveness of his On Balance Volume Indicator theory. He decided to pull up stakes and leave Wall Street.

Granville had been roaming the country looking for a good place to live. He found it in Holly Hill, Florida. In July 1963 he gave notice, moved out of New Jersey, and bought a place in

Holly Hill, where he moved his family. It was there that he founded *The Granville Market Letter*.

In a typical fictional dramatization of the life of a successful man, the final break with the Wall Street hierarchy would be the turning point in the protagonist's life. From that moment on, his luck would take an upward swing; he would have taken the final irrevocable step and proved himself right.

Not so Joseph E. Granville.

"I selected Holly Hill as a home base," he explained later, "because it is a name that sticks in people's minds. Actually, the city is a suburb of Daytona. There is nothing romantic about the words Daytona Beach. But there is about Holly Hill."

Using the same techniques he had employed when he launched his philalic investment newsletter, he began publishing his weekly communiqué to stock market investors. It was full of advice on market trends. Mostly he relied on the analytic techniques he had perfected on Wall Street—all the traditional ones—in addition to his On Volume Balance Indicator.

Results were mixed to say the least.

Along with the strictly technical indicators, Granville also believed at that time that other factors—including war or peace, boom or bust, profit or loss, even love or hate—influenced market trends. In other words, he was not then a strict technician.

Morality became an ancillary indicator that intrigued Granville. The 1960s brought about a break with the old moral values; there was a sharp increase in crime rates and in premarital sexual intercourse. There were more topless waitresses, nudie floor shows, and even nude bathing beaches. All this signaled to Granville a decline in prosperity and a return to hard times.

He called for a falling market, but as if to spite him, it continued its upward climb all through the early 1960s. Granville tried to revise his system to keep up with what he considered to be an erratic market performance. What he finally did was return strictly to the use of technical indicators rather than sentimental ones.

However, by 1971 he had hardly become a wild success in the newsletter business. He now had eight children and, ironically enough, a disintegrating marriage. He was bringing in money, but he was working hard to get it—too hard to permit his marriage to survive.

"Talk about incompatibility," he said later. He and his wife, Pauline, simply did not get along. "She would get tired at 9:30. I don't come awake until 1 A.M. She decided she didn't want me smoking in the house. I like to have a drink. She doesn't drink."

After twenty years of marriage she reportedly threw him out of the Holly Hill house. Luckily, he had opened up a small office in town, and it was there that he camped. Sleeping on the floor of his tiny one-room office, he managed to elicit a rent-free deal for a while from his eighty-three-year-old landlady, a widow with whom he was on friendly terms.

Now came an ever more bitter pill for Granville to swallow. In 1973 and 1974 the stock market was involved in wild gyrations both up and down. Generally speaking, the combination of rises and falls turned into a bear market. His predictions missed these moves completely. He lost more and more subscribers, until he was out of business as a forecaster.

He finally had to shut off the telephone in his office to save money. The only thing he could find to do was to revise his earlier textbook on the stock market, correcting it to compensate for the failures in his own forecasting, looking for the particular indicators or series of indicators that hadn't proved out during the 1960 rise.

He worked hard, trying to isolate the flaws. What had caused him to miss these crucial moves of the market? Granville looked back on those bad days with typical bemusement: "I was playing golf at the time. I had my eye on the ball, not the dot. I took my eye off that dot, the Dow Jones Industrial Average. I was playing great golf, though."

Those years were bad ones. It was not until 1977 that he began to recover. And, oddly enough, his recovery had more to do with his old love, show business, than with mathematical savvy, statistics, or even broker's intuition.

He still had friends, even though great numbers of his former subscribers had lost faith in their guru's magic. Jack Arnold, a Minneapolis broker, suggested that Granville hold a seminar for prospective clients. Granville decided that he was practically broke as it was and that he could lose little by obliging Arnold.

"Joe told everybody that the market was going to go down like the *Titanic*," Arnold related. "Then, in February 1978, he called and gave us a buy signal. We thought he was crazy, but it turned out to be the market bottom."

What had happened was exactly what Granville thought would happen . . . sometime. The 1978 market fall had indeed bottomed out. He had thought it would, and had been saying it would; now that it had happened, he was impressing the people he had just advised.

His seminars infused new blood into his business. After three of them, he found $8,000 worth of newsletter subscription orders in his mailbox at Holly Hill. He was on the way back up again.

"How did I recover?" Granville asked. "Like Elmer Gantry. The first chance I got to speak in public again I got up and confessed. I admitted my mistakes. Apparently I've been forgiven, because I haven't made a serious mistake since."

The allusion to Sinclair Lewis's famous preacher, Elmer Gantry, was not a casual one. Gantry was a spellbinder; his appearance was enough to rivet a crowd and make followers out of its constituents. Granville's seminars were creating an excitement that revived an old interest of the master's. It took him back to the days when he was a Valdes Player.

Soon he was structuring his seminars into more complex presentations than simply lectures on the stock market. They changed dramatically and almost overnight into performances. Granville began to make use of stage props, actors' shticks, and all kinds of excitement to create suspense and interest.

He wrote the theme song in which he derided the Wall Street technicians who were only taking people's money for their own use: "The Bagholder Blues." He ordered a ventriloquist's dummy constructed, and with it resurrected an old Charlie McCarthy-type act he had once performed.

Granville admitted the truth: "They're not seminars, they're shows. I was giving sermons. And they're free shows—I make my money that way!"

The seminars were promotion schemes to induce customers to buy his newsletter. He charged nothing for his performances, estimating that if only 15 percent of the audience signed up for his service, a performance would net him about $100,000. Almost immediately he began to draw huge crowds as news of his shows got around; what helped were his frequent appearances on television talk shows throughout the country.

His astute blending of salesmanship and show business produced a kind of spectacular that rivaled the performances of many big-league personalities.

A typical show might go this way:

First the lights would dim, with recorded music filling the auditorium or meeting hall—usually "The Bagholder Blues" or some other rollicking tune to catch the audience's attention. Then in would rush Granville, a breathless figure, lean and raunchy-looking, dressed in a tuxedo that didn't quite fit. With his huge long nose, large features, and unruly hair that flopped about his head like handfuls of straw, he resembled a scarecrow escaped from the cornfield.

In one hand he might lug a dummy, in the other a bag filled with puppets, bells, golf balls, and perhaps an assortment of funny underwear. And then the show would begin. Each performance would be different, scattered with quick humor, local references, and topical remarks.

His spiels usually contained pithy statements about current topics: "What do OPEC prices have to do with the market? Nothing! What do gold, hostages, and inaugurations have to do with the market! Nothing!"

But it was in his personal touches that his real dramatic talent shone through. He worked his own image to the bone.

He might grab the edges of his mouth with his forefingers and pull it wide, proclaiming, "When you look at me, you're looking at a certified fruitcake!" Long pause while the audience laughed. "But I can make you rich!"

Or he might rush out into the audience and put his hand on a beaming widow's shoulder, crying out: "Everybody I touch I make rich!"

Or he might quote the Bible: "As Matthew says, 'The Eye is the lamp of the Body.' If my eye is on the right things, the market rewards me!"

Or he might unbuckle his belt and let his pants drop to the stage in order to make a point about inflation and its effects on the wardrobe.

Usually at some point in his routine he would go into his investment sketch, explain his philosophy, and then break off into clowning, ventriloquism, and delivering devastating comments on his rival analysts and economic forecasters.

"Incompetents!" he would rage. To him, every member of that fraternity was a charlatan. Alan Greenspan was "a bespectacled prune." Louis Rukeyser became "Crab Louie." Financial writer Dan Dorfman was played by a chimpanzee named "Dwarfman." On the Phil Donahue show, Granville looked sternly into his host's eyes and told him: "Phil, you're a loser!"

Chimpanzees, monkeys, and apes were favorites with Granville. At one performance, he turned to the wings and yelled,

"Come in, bagholder!" Instantly a monkey entered, dressed in a pin-stripe suit—Granville's idea of a typical bank trust officer, stockbroker, economist, or any other bagholder. After a big laugh, the monkey walked over to Granville and began picking his pockets. More laughter. The monkey finally climbed to the top of a stepladder, grabbed a bag planted there, and carried it all the way to the bottom.

Granville worked hard on his entrances. The first principle of show business is to grab attention immediately by a striking opening. His costumes included blinking bow ties, togas, and undershorts imprinted with stock quotations. "Hell," he said, "when people are entertained, they remember three times as much as they do if they are bored stiff."

At one show in Seattle, dressed in his usual shiny, slightly awry tuxedo, he slithered down onto the stage from a 100-foot wire strung up in the wings. During the hostage crisis in Iran, he strode into the spotlight dressed like the Ayatollah Khomenei. In Anchorage, he arrived onstage in a dogsled like a leftover from the Gold Rush. He once sauntered in view dressed as a huge chicken, obviously ready for plucking by Wall Street.

In Tucson, he staged his show in an extensive outdoor arena surrounding a large swimming pool. Entering, he walked across the swimming pool on top of the water, treading an invisible slab of see-through fiberglass just below the surface. To great applause, he picked up a microphone after his wave-walk and said with a leer: "Now you know."

But there was always the main theme repeated time and time again: "Wall Street is structured to make you a loser. I want you to be a winner."

In the middle of a long string of jokes, he might suddenly shift from his arm-waving, eye-bulging, strutting romp from one end of the stage to the other, and segue into a Bible-thumping revivalist routine: "The market is a jealous God! It rewards winners and chastises losers! The Holy Bible is a record of winners and losers, and the market follows every precept in that Book—the stock market is the antithesis of man's ways. Now in Isaiah, it says that God's ways are not man's ways. And if the market does not follow man's ways, what does it follow? God's ways! Like the Good Book the market has only one message—follow me!"

There were other messages, too, usually couched in Granville's picturesque diction. "The market is like a train, and I'm the caboose. I have to follow it, using my technical analysis. If I start following something else, the coupling comes undone and the caboose goes down the hill."

Or: "The minute you put one jot or tittle of financial analysis into the market—dividends, earnings, gross national product— it's like putting water in your gas tank. Your car won't go."

Or: "You have to listen to the stock market. You can't understand the language at first. It's like learning Chinese. But when you learn the language and learn what it means, then you can listen. The market speaks. And when it speaks, you let it lead you to prosperity!"

Or: "At the top of a cycle, the market is balanced precariously on the edge of a cliff, like a car just about to go over. But if the car's not ready to go, all the shoving in the world won't move it."

And so on and so forth.

In the late 1970s, Granville was well into his act. He had built up an enormous following, mostly through hard work. His annual schedule included about 200 "investment seminars" (free translation: "shows" or "appearances"). He was logging about 150,000 miles a year. And he had built his subscription list to an estimated 13,000 subscribers by 1980. In addition to the 13,000 who paid $250 a year for the newsletter, he had added another service, the "early-warning service" for an extra $500, which provided the subscriber with a telephone call from Granville himself if instant action was needed on the market.

The stage was set for the showman to appear on yet another stage—this one Wall Street.

On April 21, 1980, the stock market was bogged down, with the Dow Jones average as low as it had been in 1978. Technicians had been looking for a rise for some time, but the market had continued to fool everyone. Granville decided that the time had come for some action.

On April 21 he invoked his early-warning system to telephone some 1,500 of his followers to "buy now." The market had bottomed out; it was time to get stocks at cut rate and ride up with the market.

Word of Granville's "early warning" hit New York almost immediately. On April 21 the market had closed with the Dow at 759.13, a two-year low. Realizing that Granville had told at least 1,500 of his admirers to buy, the money professionals got ready for a surge. They too decided to buy in.

What happened on April 22 was a stampede that pushed the stock market to one of its most impressive advances since November 1, 1978. By the end of the day, after the electric excitement of the rise, the market stood 30.72 points higher at 789.85.

Although there were doubters, it was generally conceded on Wall Street that the big rally was precipitated by Granville's advice. *Financial World* later wrote: "Nearly everyone on Wall Street believes [the rally] was sparked by a dramatic flurry of overnight telegrams to subscribers in which Granville proclaimed that the long-awaited market bottom was at hand."

Granville was immediately a controversial figure—touted as a "seer" by his followers and called "downright dangerous" by doubters on Wall Street.

"The index would have risen 10 or 12 points even if I hadn't urged my people to buy," he told a reporter modestly.

The market surge didn't stop in April. It continued through May and June, reaching 881.83 on June 27. Granville, again modestly: "If it was just my power, the market wouldn't have gone up another 100 points since then."

But Granville was not about to hide his light under a bushel. "I don't think that I will ever make a serious mistake on the stock market for the rest of my life," he told his critics. "People think that that's ego, but the market bestows that degree of authority. When it comes to the market I'm humble—the market itself—I never use words like 'I hope,' 'I think,' 'perhaps,' 'maybe.' I say 'I know.' If you follow me, you follow the market—we're interchangeable."

Nor was Granville less than sanguine about himself. "I was reading an article about the twelve most powerful men in the world," he told *Time*. "I'll bet not one of them ever moved the market 5 points in one day. I moved it 31 points."

Some market analysts credited Granville with just that power. Others pointed out that he was simply calling the changes accurately. Other analysts on Wall Street, went the word, could point with pride to equally good records. "It hasn't really been all that difficult to call the market turns over the past three or four years," one said.

Another said: "Word had gotten around that Granville was bullish. The market had been open just a short time, but I knew the four or five stocks that he recommended—Mobil was one of them—and I checked. None of them had opened. I got on the intercom, and none of them opened for at least half an hour. When they finally did, it was with gaps of 1 to 3 points."

Obviously when Granville had talked, his followers had listened.

It was the April 22 call that made Granville's name a household word with little investors across the country.

And the stage was set for the next offering in the Joseph Granville Players stock company.

In spite of the carping that went on after Granville's first big call put him into the newspapers and magazines, he continued to make his recommendations and predictions. As with all independent forecasters and analysts, he enjoyed freedom from restrictions and federal intervention that was not allowed brokers and analysts under the thumb of the Securities and Exchange Commission and subject to the ethical canons of the industry.

"The restrictions that the average analyst works under and his own discipline restrict him from writing in the manner Joe Granville does," said one senior brokerage-firm analyst. Another elaborated: "If a broker made the same claims in front of a public audience that Joe Granville does, he'd be carted off by the SEC in handcuffs, barred from the business forever, and quite probably locked up."

In fact, some murmurs surfaced in Wall Street to the effect that the SEC should crack down on Granville for some of his statements and recommendations; there were regulations that could be invoked. However, the SEC was notoriously lax on most newsletter writers, both in their publications and in their advertising.

Other analysts who were rather friendly to Granville saw a cloud on the horizon. "Right now," one of them said, "Granville is probably saving people money by getting them more in touch with the market. And as long as he's right on the market, I guess everything will be OK. I just worry that if his timing ever goes off, it could be very dangerous for a lot of people."

Another said: "If people are following Granville blindly, it's like following the Pied Piper—he could march them right over a cliff."

The cliff was suddenly there, and the Pied Piper was approaching it. From the day in April that Granville had told his troops to buy, the stock market had marched to his tune, up, and up, and up—with a few retreats to regroup. At the end of the year, in December 1980, the market still appeared bullish and strong. Granville was telling his subscribers to continue buying.

His letter dated January 3, 1981, titled optimistically "Straight Up," said in part: "Do some aggressive new buying." He specifi-

cally recommended General Motors, Cities Service, and Getty
Oil, as well as thirty other stocks.

"The market is signaling a sharp upswing ahead, and most
groups look set to respond vigorously. The most important thing
to know here is that most stocks are set to advance and the
probability states that regardless of what you buy right here, it
should be higher several weeks from now."

That letter was sent from the printers on Friday. When the
next week began, the market was still moving up. On Tuesday it
crossed the mythical 1000 mark once again—it had passed 1000
in 1972 and in 1976 but had retreated both times. The final
count for the day was 1004.69.

Now Granville had second thoughts. Explaining his actions
later, he said: "We have to be true to our theory. When the Dow
closed at the new high, a majority of our major indicators failed
to confirm that move with their own new highs. This is the first
time we've had a Dow high that wasn't confirmed by the broader
indexes and by other indicators [of volume, new highs and the
like] that follow."

In fact, other analysts had been warning about this divergence
between the blue chip Dow Jones Average and other market
indicators for several weeks. They contended that this left the
market vulnerable.

But Granville had written, quite correctly, in his Friday letter
that "50 points up was a piece of cake." However, he had assumed it would take time—perhaps a week or two. On Monday
the market was moving up again swiftly. On Tuesday Granville
saw the day's high, not the final closing, at 1013.13—and that
was at least 50 points from 963.99. "You can't call them any
better than that," he said later. And to him, the market was
saying that it was going to go down. "It was giving us a sell
signal," he said.

He hurried to his telephone. Within minutes special operators
in Florida were placing calls to investors around the world—men

and women who had paid Granville $500 for this kind of magic moment.

The message was cryptic but completely understandable to the cognoscenti: "Sell everything. Market top has been reached. Go short on stocks having sharpest advances since April."

And this after Friday's optimistic keep-on-buying letter!

In Europe, where the market opened hours earlier than in New York, investors were already phoning their brokers. U.S. stocks were already falling sharply even before Wall Street opened. The wave of selling was attributed to Granville's followers.

By the time the market opened on Wednesday in Wall Street, there was already devastation in Europe. The selling continued as the Americans got into the act. The Dow Jones Average at one point during the day was down 31 points from Tuesday's close; it ended the day off 23.80 points, at 980.89—a far cry from that magical 1000. But the drop didn't tell the whole story; the story was quantity, not quality. Over 92,000,000 shares had been sold, beating the previous all-high record of 84,000,000 in November 1980.

The selling wave reduced the value of stocks traded on the U.S. stock exchanges by $40 billion—a considerable percentage of the $1.35 trillion they were worth at the end of 1980.

Stock market analysts and brokers had been amused the previous year when Granville's bullish stance had helped propel the market into its long-awaited rise. Now, however, they were far from amused. Cries rang through the Street for Granville's head.

Not only were the professionals piqued; many of Granville's subscribers were too. Many of them were just opening his newsletter, which was telling them to buy aggressively, at the time the market was being pummeled by waves of selling inspired by their master's orders. Among the 15,000 subscribers, there were hundreds of defections; many of the faithful felt that they had been had. Many dropped their subscriptions and demanded their money back.

The Wall Street Journal suggested that the selling wave Granville seemed to have predicted might have been a self-fulfilling prophecy. How useful, the *Journal* wondered, was sell advice if sales of stock were so heavy—as they were on Wednesday—that few sellers got top dollar on their trades?

Granville had an answer. "With a growing following, some degree of self-fulfilling prophesy is inescapable. But the market's a fair game and wouldn't give a valid sell signal unless it had the intention of a major new downtrend. Even if sellers are hung up or get bad execution [of sell orders], the odds are that the market will be going down far enough that it pays to act on the recommendation."

In spite of those of his followers who abandoned him, Granville was euphoric about the market move: "It looks like we've done it again. When we call a top right to the day, it's a hole-in-one, an ace!"

Others were not so ebullient. "I would have bet a lot of money stocks would have opened higher, and they would have, except for Granville," said one investor. "A lot of people who loaded up with stocks on Tuesday would rather they'd never heard of him."

There was a great deal of grumbling and discontent in the wake of the big slide precipitated by Granville's sell order. SEC enforcement officials were approached by various friends or simply strangers.

"Why don't you shut down the exchange?" one woman asked.

The official questioned did not answer her but told a colleague later: "If people panic because of the Granville thing, my sympathies don't go out to them."

Even officials of the New York Stock Exchange said that they had reviewed trading during the day on Wednesday but didn't find anything that could be called a specific abuse by Granville.

Granville himself was amused at the whole idea of an SEC inquiry. "How can the SEC call on me? On what grounds? Doing my job? I wish they would call on me. Then the SEC would have to come out with a statement validating everything I do because they'd have to explain to everyone what I'm doing that they don't like. That's what's going to win me the Nobel Prize. I have solved the 100-year enigma, calling every market top and bottom."

For several days rumors were surfacing that the SEC had been looking into *The Granville Market Letter* and advertising used to promote it. Untrue, said Granville's lawyer. But later the SEC did speak with Granville, with little fanfare from either side.

Several Wall Street investment firms that had been sponsoring Granville's seminars began having second thoughts. E. F. Hutton, which had originally employed him, only to have him give them some unappetizing publicity, was beginning to hedge on future seminars, as was C. Bache Halsey Stuart Shields Inc., which had been actively sponsoring his get-togethers.

However, the general consensus was that Granville's sell order would be his last recommendation. "His day is over," said one E. F. Hutton executive. "He'll probably be plastered with lawsuits when it's all over." Granville, he predicted, would lose credibility among the investors whom he advised to buy stocks in his market letter on Friday but didn't contact when he delivered his sell signal Tuesday night.

Granville was not at all worried about his own reputation in regard to the plunge. "I see no problem whatsoever," he said. "I've had very little reaction from subscribers. There simply isn't any way to avoid this. It will happen at every market turn. It's like going into a movie house, paying full price, and seeing 'The End' on the screen after they're inside for two minutes. I say there'll be another movie right after that and it's called 'Bear Market.'"

Besides, he pointed out, in the two days following his advice, the Dow Jones Industrial Average went down 38.99 points to

965.70. "With or without me, the market would have gone down Wednesday, maybe not 23 points but at least 8 of 10. I'm not the ball game; I just gave it a little extra kick."

As for being through, Granville laughed off his critics: "It doesn't change my perspective one iota. When I was a child, six years old, my father took me to the top of the Empire State Building and sat me on the ledge and I looked down 102 stories. He held on to me. That's the last time in my life I ever looked down. I'm going to keep on calling market tops and bottoms whether it's for ten people or ten million."

Granville's basic optimism may have saved him from some remorseful days, but the plunge in the market, to which his name was forever attached, did not do him unalloyed good. It made his name almost a household word, no matter what kind of value judgment was attached, but it didn't help his subscriptions any. He lost almost 2,000 of them from disgruntled followers who had not been warned in time of the market drop. Others wouldn't bother to renew when their subscriptions ran out.

By the end of January, Granville's prediction had proved out. The market was down by 80 points from its high. However, without any help from him, it suddenly rebounded very smartly, exceeding its former high to reach 1024.05 on April 27.

In mid-February, Granville had made another prediction: this time that the market would drop 16 points in a big selloff. It didn't happen that way at all: the DJIA rose more than 8 points. On Februrary 27 it stood at 974.58.

But meanwhile Granville had come up with another amazing prediction that had nothing to do with the stock market at all.

At 5:31 A.M. on April 10 he said that a major earthquake of 8.3 on the Richter Scale would occur twenty-three miles east of Los Angeles (presumably the dead center of L.A., which would be the City Hall or Civic Center). And that earthquake would shear off all the land west of the epicenter, leaving the Mojave Desert excellent for surfing and Phoenix "beachfront property."

"I follow thirty-three earthquake indicators," he explained. "If you knew what I knew, you couldn't keep quiet." He said he based his prediction on worldwide seismic activity and the alignment of Jupiter, Saturn, and Mercury.

Nothing happened; it was a tranquil morning on the West Coast.

Later, when Granville was finally located after having avoided newsmen for some time, he admitted to the media that he was indeed grateful that what he had predicted hadn't happened.

But worse was yet to come. The ex-seismologist returned to his drawing board and suddenly saw another big dive in the DJIA. Reviving from its plunge out of the 900s in September, the market was making a valiant attempt to rise once again. But Granville saw technical weaknesses.

The market, he proclaimed in his newsletter, would fall once again, continuing the slide begun in January. On September 21, the Dow Jones rose 10.37 points to 846.56, but Granville was still seeing a slide, a new "Blue Monday." In his newsletter dated Friday, September 24, he predicted that the market would collapse on Monday.

He had been saying the same thing all week, and the market had responded by moving from 846.56 to 845.70, to 840.94, and then down 5.80 to 835. Everything, according to Granville, was ready for a big break.

On Monday—

At first the scenario was played out to perfection. "Blue Monday" started out exactly as Granville had predicted. The Japanese and European markets went down staggeringly. The New York Stock Exchange sank with a 16-point loss in the early hours of the day.

With this quick sinking, investors who had bought on margin and whose brokers demanded they put up more cash for stock not fully paid for were forced to sell. This quickly shook out the weak sisters. The panic subsided. Then, quite suddenly, the bargain hunters rushed in, having been tipped off in advance by Granville's predictions. There was a quick rally, and as more and more stocks were gobbled up, the gain posted turned out to be the biggest in six months. By the end of the day, the DJIA went on to post an 18.55 point rise, winding up at 842.56, almost back to what it had been at the beginning of the previous week.

On Tuesday it was up another 5.33 points, to 847.89; next day it was 849.98.

"The Swami Takes a Fall," one magazine headlined the story.

"Joe Granville may have done everyone a favor when he flatly predicted that the stock market would collapse," wrote Jack Egan in *New York*. "The New York market proved him wrong and proved itself both smarter and more resilient than he expected. . . . The stock market today is in better shape than before Granville spoke."

One broker summed it up: "It's quiet now. It sounds like not much is going on. I think even on Monday you could tell that the predictions were not going to come true. Normally you get a real lump in your throat when a selling climax comes. You feel like regurgitating, if you know what I mean."

A secretary was more unnerved: "My husband explained it to me. He said it was like if everybody on our street heard that their property values were going down and decided to sell their house, that that's what happened in the morning. And then if we decided maybe they were wrong and bought a house at much lower than it should have cost and so, when the values didn't go down, made a lot of money. That's what happened in the afternoon. The way everybody was talking yesterday, I had to know. I thought they were going to start coming out of the windows."

Granville's series of misses and the ancillary demonstrations of his fallibility tended to put him a little out of the limelight after that September fiasco. But he continued to hold his seminars and publish his newsletter. It was largely because of the fact that he had missed a few big ones that he staged his "resurrection" at Atlantic City in May.

To the faithful, Granville seemed to be using fewer of his old tricks in his presentation—in spite of the coffin and the martini. Although he claimed that the SEC was not after him, officers from the federal regulatory agencies did indeed speak to him, and several lawyers from the New York State Attorney General's office called on him as well. They discussed the January market slide. Granville was sobered by these exchanges.

What actually is Joseph E. Granville's track record? How does he compare with his fellow prognosticators? Can he be depended on?

Granville's strength is his ability to predict extreme turns in the stock market—that is, a downturn after a long upturn or an upturn after a long ride downward. His weakness is in his inability to pick specific stocks. He was right in all the big turns after 1979.

On April 22, 1980, for example, he selected eight stocks, including General Dynamics, International Paper, and Mobil. In the two months following that selection, the average of these stocks appreciated 11 percent. However, the DJIA had run from 759 to 860, an increase of 13 percent. Of the eight Granville selected, only three—Honeywell, Hughes, and Norfolk & Western—rose more than the market itself did; and they rose only by a point or two. Assuming that every subscriber had bought stocks at their April 21 price, Granville's faithful would not have made as much as those who selected stocks at random.

In January 1980 Granville was pushing General Motors as "today's lemon" that would become "tomorrow's plum" at the price of 54. In April, when the DJIA hit bottom, GM was selling at 45. "He's had some real clinkers as far as his stock picking is concerned," one Wall Streeter said. "Some of his lemons didn't turn into plums—they turned into rotten lemons."

Even in his fairly accurate calls on major market turns—he did call three of the four major market turns between 1979 through the middle of 1981—he missed a lot of the smaller twists and turns.

On January 19, 1981, he said the Dow would sink below 900 by February 23. It didn't. On February 24 he said the Dow would drop 16 points the following day. It rose 8. On March 6 he said the Dow would fall below 900 before it topped 1000. It didn't.

Even after the big selloff on January 6, 1981, Granville forecast a steady decline from the high of 1004.69; however, the market recovered to its previous high. Another of his most unfortunate lemons was his recommendation of Chrysler stock. And Bally and Caesars World, which he chose in 1980, lost more than they gained, although the rest of his gambling stock selections made out very well.

"Chrysler will be one of the outstanding moves in the 1980 stock market and you can bet on it," he wrote early in the year. Then, after March, the stock disappeared from Granville's "buy" list. However, it returned on September 20, when it was selling at 9 ⅞, and stayed there until the message to "sell everything"—by which time it was at 5 ⅞ again. When the market bottomed in April, Granville wrote a new buy list of twelve stocks. By January 1981, only Chrysler had been sold. The remaining were presumably sold on that date. Their average gain: 7.3 percent. During that same eight-month period, the DJIA rose 26.4 percent.

But Granville has an excuse for his record with individual stocks: "Market first, stocks second. Since the market is headed higher, don't become overconcerned with what stocks you are in."

True, but Granville never told his subscribers that. Nor did he ever suggest to them that they pay attention only to his market analysis and use other counselors for individual stock selections. Instead, he dismissed such elements as long-term investment, risk-management, hedging, investing for yield, and tax considerations.

"I have no message for investors," he said, "because investors don't follow the market. And the market has only one message: 'Follow me.' The market doesn't know how old you are or your tax position or your marital status or your financial status."

But Granville never told his subscribers that the obvious step to take would be to go to an investment adviser who would know the investor's individual needs.

More fuss was caused by Granville's January 1981 call than by any other prediction he ever made. The reason for the excitement was that so many people took a blood bath in the carnage caused by the turn. Did Granville cause the turn? Obviously not. But his timing in calling the slide did cause injury to many.

A rival newsletter publisher, Bert Dohmen-Ramirez, discussed the January market slide from the standpoint of forecasters other than Granville: "Over the last few months, certain nonconfirmations in the market, certain technical weaknesses, had been pointed out by ourselves and others. But not by Granville. He did not tell people, OK, take it a little easy because we're going to start approaching a top pretty soon. He kept saying to buy everything."

Granville answered the charge this way: "If you follow the market you have to follow the dictate of 'all or nothing at all.' You are not long and short at the same time."

The major difference between Granville and his competitors had always been his insistence that market timing was everything and that stock selection was unimportant. But as Stanley Weinstein, a competitor and publisher of *The Professional Tape Reader*, wrote: "When you have a very strong trend, like you had in 1975, then market timing is more important than market selection. But then there are other markets, like 1972 and 1977, where you have divergent trends and tricky markets. At those times it's sheer folly to talk about what the market is doing. In 1977 I was long secondary stock and short blue chips and glamours and did very well. I think we're in the same kind of market right now [March 1, 1981], especially since last September. Stock selection is extremely important."

Granville, of course, did not agree. "My system is as pure as it can be. I'm trusting the market. It hasn't let me down in six years."

Newton Zinder, the analyst who replaced him at E. F. Hutton, understood Granville's preoccupation with the stock market: "The market is that creation of man that has most humbled him," he said. "The ones who usually make the biggest mistakes are those who predict they will never make a mistake."

Other competitors were even more hostile: "There are clear lines separating those who swear by him and those who swear at him," said Louis Rukeyser, the pundit who hosted, and still does, a weekly TV show about Wall Street.

Even Weinstein noted, "He tells unsophisticated audiences that he'll never make another mistake and they believe him. That's dangerous."

Stockbrokers had grown even more suspicious of him: "After a Granville show, I've had people come in here and write out a check for $50,000 or $100,000 and tell me to follow Granville," one of them said after sponsoring a Granville seminar. "That's all. They don't want to know. Just follow Granville. Sure they make money. All my clients who follow Granville do. Lots of it. But it's the power Granville has that's disconcerting."

The most clear-cut argument against Granville still came from the fundamentalists. Their thesis is: "We want to buy a stock only when its price is very low relative to the fundamentals of the company." The difficulty, of course, lies in separating the fundamentals of the company's operation from the technical factors in the market that would make the price higher or lower.

"Economists and bank trust officers"—Granville meant those who leaned toward the fundamentals of the system—"don't know anything about the stock market and are not qualified to make an intelligent statement regarding the market."

In turn, the fundamentalists usually liken technical analysis like Granville's to voodoo. However, both fundamentalists and technicians believe in the Dow Theory—that when the peaks of the average rise keep getting higher, and the troughs keep getting higher, the price of stock is tending upward in a bull market, and vice versa for a bear market.

The theory also applies to individual stocks. "If you keep charts on stocks," said one technical analyst, "you know that trends will continue for months or years. If a stock is in a downtrend for two or three weeks, the chances are that it will continue for a while. I assume it stays in effect until there is evidence of a change. I don't ask questions about why it's happening."

Lately, however, the whole theory of such trends has been brought into disrepute by arguments from statisticians and mathematicians. One disbeliever, Burton Malkiel, of Princeton University, author of A *Random Walk Down Wall Street*, used an experiment to prove that the trends developed by the analysts were phantoms conjured up in their minds.

He had his students flip coins several hundred times and record the results on a stock market chart as if a "heads" were equivalent to a 50-cent rise in price and a "tails" a 50-cent fall. A chart that was prepared from these random flips was then given to a technician and he was asked to analyze it.

"I see this as a bullish market," the technician was supposed to have said. "We've got to buy immediately."

Some thinkers have pointed out that the random walk makes fundamental as well as technical analysis worthless. Data influencing prices is unpredictable, and to the extent that it is known, it has already been factored into the prices.

However, most of them concede that a fundamental approach to investment can produce payoffs. The stock market doesn't truly take all available, relevant information into account, partly because a fair number of investors simply don't have access to pertinent facts.

Nevertheless, in spite of these arguments between fundamentalists and technicians, many technicians, including Granville, had scored excellent track records over the years. To academics not in any way attached to the stock market, the law of regression to the mean would ultimately discredit high performers like Granville.

Another experiment developed by Malkiel: He had 1,000 people flip coins, declaring the "heads" flippers winners, the "tails" flippers losers. After the first flip, there were about 500 winners. The winners got to flip again, producing approximately 250 winners. In each of the rounds, the number of winners halved, or close to it. There would be about eight winners in the seventh round. By the ninth round, or tenth, one or two coin flippers, widely regarded as infallible experts, would remain.

"The laws of chance do operate," Malkiel wrote, "and they can explain some amazing success stories."

Like that of Joseph E. Granville?

After the failure of California to self-destruct and slide into the Pacific, Granville started to sober up his image, purchasing a lot of pin-stripe suits and lowering his somewhat high profile.

"We're in a bear market," he remarked by way of explanation. "People's money is on the line. They don't have a bullish sense of humor." So out with the puppets, the dummies, the monkeys, and the balloons, even the comic underwear.

By 1982 Granville was one hundred percent sure the market was going to perform a China Syndrome through the bottom of the earth—650 or even 550 by the end of the year.

"The more things come up, the more they'll come down," he told his followers. "The rallies in the bear market are always sharper than the rallies in a bull one."

He did not like the way things were shaping up politically, either. "I would not be surprised to see the recession of 1981 to 1982 usher in the depression of 1983," he noted. "Mark my

words: Ronald Reagan will be the Herbert Hoover of his generation."

He was still advising his followers to do exactly as he had
suggested in January, 1981: "Sell everything!"

And he was right about the bear market. Up to the middle of
summer, anyway. But then the market began to rise spec-
tacularly. Granville stuck to his guns. He hasn't changed his
mind even yet. He's still convinced the bottom will drop out of
everything, just like in 1929. Or so he says.

But many remember what he said shortly after he had mis-
calculated on the 1981 earthquake that was going to destroy Los
Angeles: "Who cares if I'm wrong?" he retorted after someone
asked him what he would do if the quake didn't happen. "I'll be
off the southern coast of Australia fishing and they'll never find
me. You don't think it's going to stop my fun, do you?"

3
John M. Templeton

Like Eliot Janeway, John M. Templeton was among the vanguard of 1930s economists who recognized one significant fact that had escaped a great many of their contemporary brethren. That fact, quite briefly, was that war and money are inextricably linked, and that when a country turns its forces of production toward building a war machine, the economy immediately prospers.

Templeton was only twenty-six years old when Poland was invaded by Germany in 1939. As an economics major and Rhodes Scholar just out of college, he had gone to Wall Street to try out the theories he had studied at Yale and Oxford. After two years of acclimatization, he borrowed $10,000 from his boss and began an experiment that proved dramatically successful.

The United States, just about to emerge from the Great Depression, was still involved in an economy that was greatly depressed, with currency badly deflated. Templeton had been studying in England, and his presence there during the increasing apprehension over another war—once again with Germany—led him to suspect that the United States would soon be involved in the titanic struggle to crush Adolf Hitler's territorial aspirations. He guessed that the U.S. economy would soon become prosperous, and when it did, the value of stocks would rise accordingly.

With his borrowed grubstake, he shopped around for every

U.S. stock that was selling for $1 or less. Many of them represented companies that had gone bankrupt or were in miserable straits. The war would spur the economy and his 10,000 shares of undervalued stocks would then appreciate in value.

He was correct on both counts.

Within four years his approximately $10,000 was worth almost $40,000. He had quadrupled his investment. His feat did not go unnoticed among Wall Street professionals. He was almost immediately declared a minor Wall Street legend—a boy genius who had made good.

In the early 1980s, some forty years after his initial entry into the stock market, Templeton still remained bullish about the DJIA, predicting that it would rise to 1500 in the 1980s and then to 3000.

He did not believe that the market's rise would be a steady and sure one. There would be some twists and turns before 1500 was reached: "Stocks go in cycles, in styles."

But cycles and styles, he often said, did not mean that the fundamentals were invalid. By fundamentals he meant the real values of the corporations issuing the stock. By cycles and styles he meant short-term fluctuations, which did not affect the market on its long haul over the years.

His belief in the 1980s was that stocks were once again undervalued, just as they had been in the 1930s. Stock market prices were, in the 1980s, around eight times company earnings. That meant that the total price of the stocks as valued on the market in a day-to-day reading was about eight times the total yearly profits of the company.

Historically, the ratio of price to earnings was about 14 to 1. However, during the late 1960s and 1970s, most U.S. stocks had been undervalued. According to Templeton: "This is an unusual situation. We are about ready now [in the 1980s] to experience the next great bull market."

Most fundamentalists use the price/earnings (P/E) ratio in evaluating a company's stock. The price-earnings ratio is determined by dividing the stock's price by its current annual earnings per share. Suppose a company is priced at $45 a share and the stock's earnings per share is $6.50. The P/E would be 6.92, or, rounded off, 7 to 1. (Many stock quotations regularly list the P/E ratio; if not available, it can be found in company reports or other quotations.)

Templeton's optimistic prediction was based on the fact that he felt the traditional fourteen-times-earnings average would once again assert itself. In addition, he saw the cost of living doubling within the next few years. As the cost of living went up, so would corporate earnings, doubling in the same period of time. Because of this hand-in-hand rise, stock prices would rise correspondingly as corporations raised dividends.

In the above example, the stock earning $6.50 a share normally would sell on the market at about $91 (6.5 × 14). In Templeton's view, the real value of the stock would be $91 at fair market value, not $45.

"There is a better than fifty-fifty chance that American share prices will triple in the next eight years." Templeton based his belief in such a rise on the fact that the P/E ratio was now about 5 to 1 instead of 14 to 1, one-third of the true value.

He used several key factors as bases for his prophecy:

• With the rise in conglomerates and mergers, the corporation that might take over a second company would often pay 50 to 100 percent over the market price for the stock in the acquisition. "This is bargain time," Templeton pointed out.

• Many companies were buying up their own stock to take advantage of the low prices. The remaining shareholders would benefit from these bargain buys.

• Price/earnings ratios in other nations were much higher than in the U.S. In Singapore, it was 18 to 1. In Hong Kong, 20 to 1. In Japan, 22 to 1.

• Templeton noted that replacement values were close to record lows. In other words, the stock price reflected a definite undervaluation of the assets of a company. To replace these assets at the current rates would cost many times the stock price.

"The best financial advice is to buy whatever is on the bargain counter, whatever is cheapest. Don't buy what everyone else is buying. Buy those things that are neglected or that other people are selling for some reason. Buy things that are already depressed.

"If you look very hard you can find particular bargains at the Stock Exchange bargain counter. Some stocks now sell at a price as low as two times what they may earn per share five years hence. Just remember not to buy the stocks everyone else happens to be buying."

As for the economy: "The U.S. economy will progress," Templeton said, "but not as fast as we hope. Inflation might average 9 percent for the next ten years. We can hope for a slow rate of increase in the output of goods."

Unlike the goldbugs and the collectibles investors, Templeton believed, and still does believe, the real buys to be on the Big Board. "One of the least expensive items are stocks on the New York Stock Exchange. Common stocks are 20 percent lower, on the average, than they were twelve years ago, while gold, silver, and real estate are all substantially up.

"Because stock prices are relatively low and cheap, more assets should go into bargain stocks than anything else."

John Marks Templeton was born some sixty-nine years ago in Winchester, Tennessee, "near Dogpatch," as he later put it. His father was a lawyer and cotton merchant and his mother a strong churchgoer. Even when he was a young boy, he differed from many of his friends because of his devotion to Presbyterianism.

His religious interests did not keep him from leading a normal life, nor from the ability to exploit his natural joy of life and his intellectual interests. His childhood was right out of *Tom Sawyer*. He did most of the conventional things—peddled magazines from door to door and did odd jobs down at the corner grocery store.

"We always went to Sunday school," one of his cousins recalled. "But our main occupation was hunting and swimming in the Elk River. Everyone knew John would be successful. When he'd read a book there was no *way* to break his concentration. And, boy! could he win arguments. Not because he was stubborn, but because he was usually right and knew it."

His schoolwork was so good that it was obvious he was destined for a college education, and he worked hard to get grades good enough to put him in Yale. He was accepted in 1930, but trouble struck immediately.

His father was almost wiped out by the Depression, and never fully recovered. The cotton business was dead and his law firm was on hard times.

"That was one of my luckiest breaks," Templeton recalled, "because it taught me very quickly to rely on myself." It wasn't easy, but he put himself through college on money earned from odd jobs and various scholarships.

The lessons of his own genteel poverty had taught him an appreciation of finance: "I decided that if I was going to do something to benefit the world, I needed something to buy groceries first."

It was while in college that Templeton discovered that there was very little information available to help the average person invest his or her money the right way. Most stock market investors were rich men or women who had their own experts taking care of their portfolios or were foundations for the extremely rich run by professional managers.

What Templeton realized was that there was no information available to the little investor—who, after all, was the backbone of the country's stability. How could such persons determine the worth of a company in which they wanted to put money?

"I decided to study to become a specialist in what a corporation is *really* worth," he said. "Then as now there were wide differences between what stocks were *really* worth and their market prices. I was fascinated by the difference."

His new career didn't begin right away. He had become such a gifted student that he earned a Phi Beta Kappa key and graduated second in his class at Yale in 1934. In addition to these honors, he also was appointed a Rhodes Scholar. Before settling down to business, he traveled to Oxford to study for two years after graduation.

On $450 he had saved during his years at Yale and Oxford, he made a seven-month tour of thirty-five European nations. It was his modern version of the nineteenth century's Grand Tour. What Templeton saw frightened him; now more than ever he knew war was in the offing.

True to his nature, he recouped half of the $450 he put out for his travels by writing an article on the trip for *Good Housekeeping*.

He then returned to America, preoccupied by the obvious danger of another global war, but unable to let it deter him from his already determined course. He was going to work on Wall Street.

He got a job in research at Fenner & Beane (later Merrill Lynch Pierce Fenner & Smith, Inc.). He worked there for two years.

"When I went into Wall Street, it had just gone through its greatest depression. In the class of 1929 at Yale, over 50 percent of the graduates went into Wall Street; seven years later less than 10 percent did. Well, 1937 was the year to go in, not 1929."

He spent his time learning market analysis and watching his fellow employees at the investment company. And as he worked he observed carefully what was going on in Wall Street.

He noticed that, generally speaking, most security analysts tended to run in packs: they tended to follow the stock market in its trends rather than lead it the way a pheasant shooter leads the pheasant.

"Whenever twelve security analysts agree, you can be sure the decision is wrong," he said, "because their opinions are already reflected in the market prices."

Templeton also noticed that money analysts overlooked one important factor: they rarely hunted for bargains. He had grown up in a family that had to hunt bargains in order to survive. When a pack of analysts grabbed up certain stocks, they drove up the prices, leaving others floundering at lower prices. Templeton decided that a bargain hunter had a first-class opportunity to buy a good stock at a low price and ride it up as it improved.

He was convinced that the stock market was going to go up. One important factor that led him to this conclusion was the growing threat of war in Europe. His tour had convinced him that there was going to be a big war that would eventually entangle the United States as well. And even if it didn't involve the U.S., America would make money supplying arms for the combatants. He concluded that the stock market, which had been floundering for ten years, would go up.

To test his theory, he borrowed $10,000 and wound up with $40,000. At about the time Templeton made this successful foray into investment, a friend whom he had met at Oxford—George C. McGhee, also a Rhodes Scholar—got in touch with him and persuaded him to move to Dallas as an officer in an investment firm. A geophysicist, McGhee was independently wealthy; he later became a multimillionaire oilman and U.S. ambassador to West Germany under Lyndon Johnson.

"I saved half my salary," McGhee told Templeton, "and when I had a chance to buy an investment counseling business for $6,000 in 1940, I had the money."

Templeton took McGhee's advice and moved to Dallas. He did better than McGhee. Later, when he sold the shares in National Geophysical in 1942, Templeton came away with $100,000.

That was the year he began studying under Benjamin Graham at New York University. Graham was a securities analyst who had an uncanny knack for evaluating stocks and bonds. He taught at least 100 different criteria to gauge a stock's true value.

"I studied under Ben Graham," Templeton said, "who did more than any man I know of to make security analysis a science."

As the end of World War II came into sight in 1945, Templeton decided that the best bargains were not going to be in United States offerings—they were at that time valued at par or even overvalued because of the rising stock market—but in European stocks. After all, Europe was an exhausted, war-torn area. The Marshall Plan was beginning to pump money into the resuscitation of the Old World, largely because U.S. business considered the half-destroyed countries as excellent future markets.

Templeton's heavy purchases of European stocks paid off handsomely. He was about to become one of the enormously successful legends in the stock market analyst business, a man *Forbes* called "one of the handful of true investment greats in a field crowded with mediocrity and bloated reputations."

Templeton developed the kind of investment company that would utilize his market expertise. The type he found most conducive to his talents was the mutual fund, whose popularity and growth in the postwar years was unmatched.

A mutual fund is a financial service, with one certificate—share—representing a managed interest in many companies and industries. It differs from a savings bank, which provides security for the lender's dollars with an opportunity to earn a specified amount of interest until the money is withdrawn.

A mutual fund differs from a typical brokerage company that buys specific shares of specific stocks determined by the investor and the broker in conjunction. In the mutual fund, the investor has no idea which stock or stocks are going to be considered from day to day.

A mutual fund, unlike the savings bank, doesn't guarantee a fixed number of dollars when and if the investment is liquidated. The sole business of a mutual fund, also called an open-end investment company, is to invest the shareholders' money in securities of corporations that the manager believes will make the most profits.

Instead of dealing with one specific stock, or two or three, the shares are spread out over a number of different offerings—a pool of stocks, actually, In 1868, when the first fund came into being in London, its prospectus declared that it had been formed to provide "the investor of moderate means the same advantages as the large capitalists, in diminishing the risk of investing in Foreign and Colonial Government stocks, by spreading the investment over a number of different stocks." The company was called the Foreign and Colonial Government Trust.

Immediately the idea spread, and several mutual funds appeared in America. The early 1920s provided the mutual fund as we know it today. That prototype included the typical diversification, an uncomplicated capital structure, a published portfolio, the self-liquidating feature, and prudent investment policies and restrictions. Number One in America was Massachusetts Investors Trust, 1924. By 1929, there were nineteen open-end funds. Growth languished during the Depression years; by 1940 the combined assets of mutual funds were less than $500 million.

Then came a spectacular spurt of growth, particularly after World War II had ended. People who had lost money in the 1929 crash mistrusted individual stockbrokers now. But there was safety in numbers. With ten stocks, one wouldn't lose everything, as in 1929. Besides, balancing and playing the percentages was a better way to play a winning game, even if the individual profits might not be quite so spectacular.

By the end of 1972, total assets had mushroomed to $60 billion, with more than 10,000,000 shareholders.

When Templeton began his dealings in the market, mutual

funds were still in their infancy after their arrested beginnings in the 1920s. However, once America found itself prosperous at the end of the war, money began pouring into the stock market, where the value of investments was increasing dramatically.

Somehow the concept of a pool of investor money appealed to Templeton's instincts. He knew how a man like his father could lose everything with a decisive swing of one particular stock or type of investment.

There are a number of advantages the typical mutual fund has over individual investment portfolios:

• It spreads the investor's dollar over many different types of stocks and securities. A disaster in any one or few of them does not mean the end of the fund. A typical fund might have $1 billion invested in more than fifty stocks, none of which would account for more than 5 percent of the fund's total market value at any one time.

• One of the most important features of the mutual fund for the beginning investor was (and remains) the much smaller amount of money needed to start an account than is needed for a typical portfolio. Most brokers don't want to work with people interested in investing only $100. The typical mutual fund investment was once as low as that. The $100 investor could then add in smaller amounts at any time to increase his or her share.

• The purchaser of a share in a mutual fund can buy a pro rata share of many different corporations in a number of different industries. An individual investor has to go to considerable trouble to realize such an excellent diversification, not to mention the enormous commission expenses involved. Because a mutual fund purchases stocks in such large quantities, it always qualifies for minimum sales-commissions, cutting down the expense for each shareholder.

• The purchaser of a share in a mutual fund benefits from the expertise of a full-time money manager who watches over the fund's portfolio from day to day and makes all the necessary decisions as to what to buy, sell, or hold. A manager might make a mistake, but in general the leading funds were and are run by people with substantial investment experience. This causes the investor to feel secure about his or her money.

• The mechanics of owning a share in a mutual fund are much less bothersome than those of owning a specific stock, with proxies to sign, rights to exercise, decisions to make, and other complications. Besides those problems, the details of filling out tax forms are simplified. A mutual fund provides information to each investor as to the total dividends and other distributions made during the year, along with tax information. On a day-to-day basis, the status and value of a mutual fund account can be determined by a glance at newspaper quotations.

• An investor might be induced to make an error under the influence of well-motivated but poorly informed friends. Lacking expert knowledge, he or she might make investment decisions on the basis of headlines, rumors, and the fears and emotions of the moment. The purchaser of a good mutual fund can sit back, relax, and let the money flow in. The time and effort needed to select and follow a good fund, compared to that required to keep track of individual stocks, are 1 to 100.

• Dividends are automatically converted to additional shares, compounding the original investment, whereas the owner of two or three stocks comes up with a handful of interest checks of such modest size that the yield could be frittered away without blinking an eye. An individual investment might lose the benefit of compounded interest. The reinvestment feature of the mutual fund is a form of enforced savings, and could make a large difference in income over several years of investment.

• Most of the larger investment companies sponsor a variety of mutual funds that offer a broad range of objectives, services, and programs. A shareholder whose investment goals have changed may be able to switch part or all of his or her principal from one fund to another within the same family of investments. In addition, this exchange can usually be done by mail, telegram, or telephone. The exchange privileges are only one of the number of shareholder services that make mutual funds an increasingly useful adjunct to financial planning. Tax-sheltered retirement plans and systematic investing and withdrawal plans are other features, making it a comprehensive and convenient investment for the individual of moderate means.

• The track record of any mutual fund can be checked out. Information as to their performances is continually published and is readily available. The amateur with money to invest can read the prospectus and shareholder reports, compare one fund with another, and make a decision as to which to buy. An individual investor has no such advantage dealing with a bank trust department or a stockbroker.

To sum up, the number of advantages—division of risk, low startup, professional management, freedom from bookkeeping, freedom from emotional involvement, automatic reinvestment of income dividends, instant and wide diversification, and readily available information on fund records—made and make the mutual fund one of the most modern and convenient versions of investment.

It was definitely the kind of investment concept that Templeton understood intuitively. He knew that it was the way he wanted to go. He decided to take the plunge.

In 1954 Templeton formed his first mutual investment fund: the Templeton Growth Fund. He was interested in foreign stocks more than in American ones for reasons already noted, and so headquartered his new fund in Canada rather than in the United

States. He used his own investment counseling company to manage the funds, working from his New York office.

His selections raised the eyebrows of many of his contemporaries. What startled them was that Templeton had put 76 percent of his stocks in Canadian companies. However, his investment analysis was correct. Canada boomed in the 1950s, making use of its immense resources.

In the 1960s he again showed his astuteness by buying up airlines stocks just as the companies were starting to purchase jetliners to take the place of the by then outmoded propeller planes. Once again his contemporaries thought he was going too far. Generally speaking, most of the smart money was not being put into an endeavor that seemed fated to destroy not only airlines but the airplane manufacturers as well.

His prescience paid off. The advent of the jetliner revolutionized the airlines industry and put it on a paying basis, involving almost anyone who wanted to travel rather than a select few businessmen.

Once again Templeton proved that his ideas were flexible enough to help him through any international crisis. In the middle 1960s, Vietnam became the focal point of international tension. Most eyes were on the American intrusion in Asian politics.

Not many people were paying much attention to China, but Templeton was. In 1965, during the height of the Vietnam explosion, China invaded India. Almost overnight, British tea stocks plummeted on the London Stock Market. Templeton felt that the Chinese would never advance into the plains of India, where the tea was grown. He reasoned that the crops would not be destroyed or diverted to China.

He bought the low-priced stocks on the assumption that the price would rise as soon as the crisis was over. He was right. The Chinese advance stopped, there was a great deal of flurry, and then the Chinese moved out of India. Immediately the stocks bounced back up. By the time they were back to normal, Templeton was able to sell them, making a tidy fortune for himself and his investors.

In the 1960s and early 1970s, Templeton kept going against the usual trends, putting his money in Japanese stocks, which at one time accounted for 62 percent of his fund's assets. Geopolitics was changing once again, and he had his attention on the market. In the late 1970s he began to see that the bargains weren't in internationals anymore, but were concentrated in U.S. stocks. The market had taken a drubbing in the 1960s and early 1970s, and because of that, stocks were underpriced once again, as they had been in the late 1930s.

By December 1980, Templeton's portfolio was 60 percent American, with heavy investments in Australia, Canada, Japan, and the Netherlands.

From the first, his investment prowess was enormously successful. He balanced his portfolios skillfully, using many European and then Far Eastern stocks, purchasing them low and trading them high. But the secret of his success was diversification.

"Never forget to diversify," he once said. "Diversification of assets is essential, of course. But because stock prices are relatively low and cheap, more assets should go into bargain stocks than anything else."

At another time, he said: "If you are going to do your own investing, don't have fewer than ten stocks. If you are going to let a mutual fund do it for you, don't have fewer than two or three. Pick the twenty-five top-performing funds for the last ten years and find three that suit your purposes. Over the next ten years that would produce a better record than any other way I know."

Those were words that could have been his own guiding light during those crucial years after World War II. His religious beliefs were a tremendous help to him. "Because John felt that God was with him," one associate said, "he invested with incredible boldness; the results make me think that maybe he's right, maybe God *is* with him."

Templeton's greatest asset was his self-confidence. That, coupled with his excellent judgment, made him almost invincible. To Templeton, self-confidence meant "Belief in and harmony with the Creator." He never could forget Ralph Waldo Emerson's advice to skeptics: "Though abyss open under abyss, and opinion displace opinion, all are at last contained in the Eternal Clause: If my bark sink, 'tis to another sea."

His track record with Templeton Growth Fund was astonishing. Anyone who had put $10,000 into the fund in 1954, and reinvested all the dividends, would have come out twenty-five years later with $276,000—a compound annual return of 14.2 percent. Templeton's closest competition in the mutual funds was Mutual Shares, which returned 13 percent.

There were many reasons for his success. "John never ran with a pack," said John Schroeder, who once managed Templeton's New York investment counseling firm, Templeton, Dubbrow & Vance. "He was a loner. But he was right. Around 1960 I ran a financial seminar. We had a Federal Reserve official who explained how the international financial system worked, and John stood up and said flatly we'd be off the gold standard in ten years and that currencies would float within fifteen, and that the U.S. dollar would weaken. It was heresy, of course. And of course he was right. Then, around 1968, when the market was selling around 1000, he came out and said it would sell below 600 in the early 1970s. Everyone laughed when John began investing overseas."

There were plenty of 600 days in 1974.

One analyst looked back on the success of the Templeton Growth Fund and partially explained it: "Reason: when the stock market in one country turns sour, he moves his chips to more ebullient markets elsewhere. In 1971, for example, 50 percent of Templeton Growth's assets were invested in Japan and 15 percent were invested in Canada. At no time before 1978 did Templeton have a majority of his portfolio invested in the U.S."

Then, when the U.S. stock market turned down in 1978, dropping into the 700s, Templeton pulled his money out of foreign funds and began to invest in American stocks. Again all the experts shook their heads. But he knew why he was doing: "I look for bargains. And the time to buy at bargain prices is when the news is so terrible that everyone is selling and driving down prices. In general, American stocks are now bargains [1978]. They are selling much lower than usual in relation to earnings, dividends and book values. They are far lower than stocks of most other countries of the world. Over the last seventy years American stocks have sold at an average of about fourteen times earnings. Singapore, France, Germany, even Sweden and London—all are higher than the U.S. And in Japan, they sell at 26 times earnings!"

There was nothing really revolutionary about his investment philosophy. It was simply a method of applying a consistent formula to a volatile situation. He did what he said he would do: he purchased growth companies when they were priced cheaply and sold them when they had appreciated in value. He bought, diversified, and then diversified again. Then, when any stock reached a realistic price, he would sell out rather than stay with it. His whole philosophy was based on a distinction that Benjamin Graham had taught him: that between a stock's inherent value and the price the market put on it at any given moment.

The reason he never held on to a stock once it had reached a realistic price was the key to his theory. "On the up side, when you are selling," he said, "I have never found any way to judge how high enthusiasm can push a stock when it has gone above what it is really worth. The ceiling is when the public stops buying, and it is hard to judge that."

Someone once asked Templeton what a good bargain was if the stock market never recognized it as such. "Suppose it was so neglected and unknown that it continued to sell at three times earnings," he responded. "Over any three years, earnings would double, and if it still sold at a multiple of three, the market price would double. Why would you ever want to sell it?"

Templeton's technique was to sell when the stock reached a price/earnings multiple of 16. "Get in when things look terribly bad; get out when they look wonderfully good." A corollary to that rule: "Buy from bored investors and sell to excited ones."

The best way for an investor to learn something from Templeton would be to buy into one of his mutual funds. By 1960 he had two under his own name—the Templeton Growth Fund and the World Fund—and managed others.

Through the years, he has evolved a number of rules of thumb. Here are a few, with his explanations and interpolations:

ON BARGAINS

"Find the best bargains you can. That means the lowest possible prices in relation to what the stock will earn. The first thing to look at is the price of a share in relationship to present earnings. Then estimate how fast those earnings are going to grow so that you can see how low the price is in relation to future earnings."

He elaborated: "When I say that a stock is a bargain, I mean that if you hold it throughout an entire market cycle you're likely to do well with it because you're getting it cheap. It *doesn't* mean we're at a favorable point in the [market] cycle. The only thing I know for certain about bull and bear markets is that *both* will occur." Templeton's advice parallels closely J. P. Morgan's answer to a question by an eager investor: "What will the market do?" He said: "It will fluctuate."

ON DIVERSIFICATION

No investor, Templeton believes, should put all his money into stocks. "At least one-third should be in something else, and most of that should be in real estate." But it still depends on the situation at the time. "I went to my bank fifteen years ago and bought 5,000 silver dollars for $5,000. Now I could sell them for $15 or more each."

Most investors and money managers, Templeton believes, make money only in bull markets, if at all, and rarely if ever outperform the market. That is because the typical going market theory holds that a stock's price reflects all the information and judgments about it and therefore indicates what it is really worth. Switching from one stock to another and searching for bargains is futile. The best way to play the market is to buy a cross-section—an index fund—and let the long-term trend carry you along.

ON THE PRICE/EARNINGS RATIO

Templeton believes that the current price/earnings ratio (1983) at perhaps 8 to 1 will likely move back to its 14 times average ratio as investors begin to pull out of cash and bonds for common stocks. That would mean that a $100 stock now earning $9 could be worth about $250 within eight years.

He believes that earnings will keep up with inflation, which he expects to average about 9 percent. If they can do that, stocks will come back into favor. People will use them as a hedge against inflation and will pay the price to own them. However, he refuses to predict a new bull market.

ON GOLD

Templeton doesn't advise anyone to buy gold. "Governments are historically prejudiced against gold owners. When Franklin D. Roosevelt became President in 1933, for example, one of his first acts was to make owning gold illegal. Everyone had to turn over his gold to the government at $20 an ounce. Roosevelt then reset the value of gold at $35 an ounce."

The last time Templeton dealt in gold was in 1974, before it took its amazing flight into the skies—and then came back to earth with a thud.

"I considered gold because it did look like a bargain. The trouble was, it was *less* of a bargain than the common stocks I was finding. And it pays no dividends."

In 1979 he said, "If I had been smart I would have bought gold a year ago, but I'd sell that now, too. The price of gold is not subject to evaluation, and I have to make an evaluation and buy the stocks that are the cheapest. But there is no way to make an evaluation of what gold is worth. It is worth whatever the psychology says its worth."

It is interesting to note that Templeton called for a sell on gold just as the boom and bust was in the wings waiting to happen.

ON ANALYZING MARKET TRENDS

"I never ask if the market is going to go up or down, because I don't know; and besides, it doesn't matter. I search nation after nation for stocks, asking: 'Where is the one that is lowest priced in relation to what I believe it's worth?' Nowhere do I ask if the market is going up or down. Forty years of experience have taught me you can make money without *ever* knowing which way the market is going."

ON OIL

"The big oil companies are very cheap in relation to their breakup values. I own more where the parts couldn't be sold for at least twice what their stock sold for in the market. But that alone would not be enough for me to buy them. Added dividends of good management and cheap price/earnings ratios—about six—did the trick."

"I wish I had bought Mexican stocks two years ago [1977] because they are up about five times. But if I had, I would sell out now [1979]. Like Japan, there is too much excitement and volume and everyone is thinking about getting rich."

ON SHOPPING GLOBALLY

Templeton believes in investing all over the world and always has. "The investor should look in every country to find assets that are selling at ridiculously low prices. But I would think that the wisest things for the average investor would be to buy shares of mutual funds managed by experts in other nations."

ON SELLING

There is no fixed rule on making the decision to sell a stock. "Over the years our funds have held stocks for an average of five years." Templeton never sells a stock and replaces it with another unless he finds that the new one represents a 50 percent better value in terms of future earnings-potential than the one he is going to sell. "Thousands of people trade their stocks too frequently, and that is a very bad mistake."

ON GETTING RICH SLOWLY

"The people who have gotten rich quickly are also the ones who got poor quickly. Ninety-nine percent of investors shouldn't try to get rich too quickly; it's too risky. Try to get rich slowly."

ON BEING RIGHT

"The very nature of investing is so difficult that you can't expect to be right more than about two-thirds of the time at best."

ON THE U.S. DOLLAR

Templeton occasionally has speculated in foreign currencies. During the middle 1970s he reaped rich rewards shorting Canadian dollars. It was only natural, therefore, that he then decided it would be wise to go along on U.S. dollars, although he never speculated himself. Theoretically, as the economy rises, the dollar rises with it.

ON TOTAL RETURN

The goal of any investor is to produce the greatest possible total return—income plus capital gains. No matter how old an investor is, he or she will still be wise to invest for capital growth rather than high dividends. "The most promising stocks usually pay out little or nothing."

ON WORLD POLITICS

Templeton tries to avoid investing in conspicuously vulnerable industries in countries that are being turned into socialist states.

ON INFLATION

For the investor in the stock market, inflation is not necessarily the worst thing in the world. The idea is to look at stocks of corporations that have a lot of debt, so long as they are not likely to run into a financial crisis. "Inflation will allow them to pay off their debts later with money that is easier for them to earn."

In the late 1960s, Templeton had suddenly had enough of the New York scene. Although he lived in a comfortable house in New Jersey, he decided to sell his home, sell his business, and move to Lyford Cay in the Bahamas. He was at that time worth about $5 million.

The Templeton Investment Counsel was the actual owner and manager of the Templeton Growth Fund and the Templeton World Fund. Templeton sold the Counsel for a handsome amount, but retained control of the main funds. Then he moved with his wife, Irene, to the Bahamas. She was his second wife. His first, Judith, had been killed in a motorbike accident in Bermuda in 1951.

The three Templeton children, John Jr., Anne, and Christopher, were by that time growing up and needed a guiding hand. Through Irene the children grew up into extremely successful professionals. John Jr. became a pediatric surgeon in Philadelphia; Anne a surgeon in Tucson. Christopher became the leader of a charismatic religious community in Jamestown, North Dakota.

Life in Nassau was good to the Templetons.

They built the house of their dreams, a neoclassical villa, white inside and out, with Southern mansion-type columns on all four sides in the style to which Templeton was accustomed in his youth in the South.

They settled into the life easily at White Columns, although Templeton was not able to shake himself of his rigorous habits. Always a man who lived life by the clock, he continued to do so, bathing daily in the ocean near the house at eleven o'clock every morning. A nonsmoker and a rare drinker, he opened an office in Nassau to which he goes regularly every day at the appointed hour.

"I don't like to upset people," he once explained, "so all my life I've attempted to be ten minutes early."

The move south was not made to take advantage of tax shelters. Templeton's interest in religion had been gnawing at him for some time.

"As my investment work prospered and I was able to get away from the day-to-day urgencies, I decided to devote half my time to helping myself and everyone else grow spiritually."

As a boy he had noticed that most adults ignored religion. "In business we appropriate $40 billion a year to research," he pointed out. Yet the churches were beginning to deteriorate, and when they did, "all humanity suffers from the belief that God is static."

Templeton had originally decided that his growing fortune would be used to fund a prize, awarded at his death, for religious progress, to be called the Templeton Prize for Progress in Religion. He wants to be remembered as "one who influenced educated people to wake up to religion."

But when he retired, he changed his mind. He wants to see for himself how it would work out and not leave it to chance. In Nassau, he set up the Templeton Foundation in order to provide money as a reward for innovators in religion.

And so the Templeton Foundation began disbursing the prize money while its founder was still alive to see his wishes realized.

He modeled the prize on the Nobel Peace Prize—with one notable difference: "I thought Alfred Nobel had a blind spot when he made no provision for religion. What was needed was a prize larger than his to say that spiritual growth is most important of all."

The purpose was to recognize persons who had done the most to advance religious thought, who had achieved something of a spiritual, not solely humanitarian, nature. To illustrate the difference, Templeton explained: "If a church founds a hospital, that is something humanitarian; but if a hospital founds a church, that is spiritual."

At first he decided to limit the prizes to Christians. But he was soon convinced that he should open the gates to all religions, on the very Christian concept that God does no less.

"If some of God's children worship Him in different ways, we shouldn't be so self-centered as to think they are wrong," Templeton elaborated. "Just as it is my duty to take the Christian Gospel and explain it to a Buddhist, so is it his duty to take the beauties of his religion and explain them to me."

One stipulation he insisted on was that there be no posthumous awards: "If we opened it up to dead people, nobody alive would ever win." The recipients had to include both sexes and varied racial and religious backgrounds. Also, a scientist had to be selected once every five years.

Templeton regarded scientific inquiry as a particularly productive avenue toward understanding God's creation. "The astronomers have taught us that there are 100 billion other galaxies and that we are no more important than any of them—all of which teaches us how infinite God is and how temporary we are," Templeton said.

The first prize paid $50,000—a lot of money in 1972, more than the Nobel Peace Prize. It went to Mother Theresa of Calcutta. Mother Theresa was the founder of the Missionaries of Charity. She won the Nobel Peace Prize in 1979.

Other early winners were Sarvepaili Radhakrishnan, a Hindu who had been former President of India, and Nikkyo Niwano, a Buddhist who had been a noted Japanese religious leader.

Another recipient was Professor Ralph Burhoe, an author-scientist and founder of the learned journal *Zygon*. Brother Roger, a member of the ecumenical Taize Community in France, was the winner in 1974. Professor Thomas Torrance, president of the International Academy of Religion and Sciences in Scotland, who had worked for nearly two decades for the reconciliation of religious and scientific thought, was the recipient in 1978. Dame Cicely Saunders, the originator of the modern hospice movement, which provides homelike service and personal attention to the terminally ill, won the prestigious award in 1981. The next year Billy Graham, founder and president of the Billy Graham Evangelistic Association in Minneapolis, received the prize. In 1983 it was the poet Aleksandr I. Solzhenitsyn who received the prize.

The current prize is $220,000; Templeton escalates the amount on a par with the rate that inflation increases the price of food and goods. There are two reasons he awards money as a prize: as an incentive to others to start something new in religion and because big money gets publicity.

"We want to say to the world that progress in religion is more important than progress in anything else. Whenever we hear of a prize that is larger than ours, we increase ours."

The prizes are awarded by the Reverend Wilbert Forker, a Methodist minister from Belfast, Ireland, who once served as a press officer for the World Council of Churches. Forker's job is to compile a list of thirty-six candidates each year. With his staff at the foundation—a group of researchers and seven trustees—he prepares dossiers on each finalist.

The files are then sent to nine international judges who go through the list and throw out thirty of the candidates. Then the judges vote on the remaining candidates by mail. Each year the judges change; they are a most select and eclectic group.

Among them have been such widely known figures as the Dalai Lama, Queen Fabiola of Belgium, Senator Mark Hatfield, Edmund Leopold de Rothschild, Gerald Ford, and Yehudi Menuhin.

Although the very differences in the backgrounds of the judges might suggest a difficulty in arriving at a consensus of opinion, such is usually not the case. "We are all searching for the same values," Menuhin remarked. "Religion keeps us in touch with the universal."

Templeton never acts as a judge; instead, he helps his staff collect information on and appraisals of the candidates.

Templeton and his wife travel all over the world interviewing the judges and finding out all they can about the candidates. This information in turn is relayed to the Foundation staff for inclusion in the dossiers being prepared on the candidates. Sometimes the biographies run to fifty or sixty pages. The judges largely depend on these dossiers for their decisions.

From the beginning Templeton envisioned the presentation of the award as a media event. And in order to make it memorable, he locates it in the most prestigious and publicity-oriented settings possible.

And so, from 1972 on, the yearly Templeton Prize for Progress in Religion has been presented either at Buckingham Palace or Windsor Castle. Prince Philip makes the presentation. The prominence of the nine judges helps fix in the public mind the prestige of the award: "Their reputation will cause the news to be picked up by television and the newspapers," Templeton explains.

Templeton is of course one of the major contributors. Others donate, but his contribution often dwarfs the rest. One year he and his wife gave 100 percent of their income. Templeton has plenty of money to enjoy himself, however; he lives well off interest and capital gains.

"By calling attention to the exciting spiritual discoveries being made," he said recently, "we hope to influence colleges, churches and individuals to set up endowments for religious research." Templeton believes that scientists today are learning more about God in their search for knowledge than they have for many years, and may be making substantial strides in uncovering the infinite facts of the spiritual universe.

A member of the Princeton Theological Seminary for thirty-two years, Templeton spent eight of them as chairman, an experience to which he attributes much of his own spiritual growth.

He has always opened the meetings of his mutual fund with a prayer, which prompted many shareholders to speak to him at the end to promise that they intended to start thinking about the deeper aspects of life. "Of course, we don't pray that our stocks will go up; we pray because it makes us think more clearly."

Templeton explains: "I tell them that prayer won't take time away from their business enterprises, but that it will help them to do *better* in business. If you are happy about your own relationship with the world and with God, you are less likely to be caught up in mistakes such as envy and greed."

His investment philosophy is steeped in religion: "I think God wants all of us to be wealthy and use our prosperity for good purposes. If He puts assets in our hands, it's our duty to make the best use of them."

Templeton's track record with his Templeton Growth Fund is easily visualized—and it is a dramatically convincing one. An investor who put $10,000 in the Fund in 1972 would have found the original investment worth $15,423 by the end of the year. Since the market took a drubbing in 1973, the original investment—with capital gains and income dividends reinvested—would have come to only $13,892 on December 31, 1973. The next year was a worse one for the market, with the total value only $12,216. But in 1975, the market turned for the better, making the $10,000 worth $16,808 at the end of the year, $24,664 the following year, $29,690 at the end of 1977, $35,393 on December 31, 1978, $44,892 at the end of the eighth year, $56,514 at the end of the ninth year just before another slump in 1981, which ended with $56,378, down a few dollars. However, the yield on the original $10,000 over the ten-year period would have been $46,378, or a straight 46.38 percent per year.

Compare that record with an investor who bought $10,000 worth of Dow Jones Industrial stocks in 1972. At the time, the market average was 890.20. Assuming that the average dividend would be somewhere in the neighborhood of 4 percent, the total dividend yield for the ten years would have come to $4,000. Assuming the average stock cost $100, the 100 shares originally purchased at 890.20 would have depreciated in Dow value to 875.00, where the market stood on December 31, 1981, a difference of $15.20 per share. That would make a loss for the $10,000 of $1,520 in the total market value of shares. Balancing the $4,000 in dividends against the loss in value of $1,520, the total gain for the ten years would be $2,480, a gain of $24.80 per year.

In other words, $10,000 in Templeton's fund would have gained $46,378; $10,000 in a composite average of industrial stocks would have gained $2,480, or about one-eighteenth of the mutual fund amount.

Templeton recently predicted that there was a fifty-fifty chance that the Dow Jones Industrial Average would reach 3000 in about five years. With the stock market wallowing in some distress at the time he made his pronouncement, there was a bit of surprise in economic circles.

There shouldn't have been, given his predilection for searching out bargains. He pointed out that the market was notoriously underpriced at the time. The current Dow rate was around 830 when he made his statement. Templeton noted that it had been in several recent months—three times, in fact—above 1000. The dynamics of the market were generally up, even though the figures were nowhere near the 1000 level.

A study of the replacement costs of the assets of the thirty companies making up the Dow average revealed to Templeton that those costs were 20 percent *less* than the combined book values of the companies. That meant that the costs would be 70 percent above the combined book values.

Translated into stock market terms, those replacement costs for the thirty companies would amount to 1700; that is, the Dow would be at about 1700 to reflect accurately the company values. The Dow quotation at the time Templeton was speaking was about half that.

To Templeton, that fact signaled extremely valuable bargains in market shares. In fact, prices seemed to him to be even lower in comparison to bargains available on the stock market after the 1929 crash, when the market plummeted from 360 to 42.

However, Templeton cautioned that he was speaking about long-term investments rather than short-term ones. It was, he said, possible that the market might sink 20 percent more before prices started to rise.

Generally speaking, he was sanguine about the economy as a whole. He felt that there would be no general depression like the Great Depression. He continued to buy with confidence in 1982, picking up bargain shares not only in the U.S. but overseas as well. He searched for the following:

• Companies quoted well below indicated values. Some of his shares were selling for as little as twice current earnings, although the average price/earnings ratio in the Fund was running "about 5."

• Stocks in companies with what he called a "surprise growth rate." To Templeton, such a rate would be at least twice that of an average company.

• Stocks that would give a better return on assets—about half as much again as the average for all companies.

• Wider-than-average profit margins.

In order to find out how a company's prospects looked, Templeton used to spend a great deal of his time investigating the management of each company individually. However, he discovered that he could learn much by "looking at the numbers" and judging the management by the track record of the company: "Ultimate performance really means more than the way the executives dress."

In spite of Templeton's good track record, and in spite of his confidence in the future of the U.S. economy, few of his competitors on Wall Street share his views on a 3000 Dow Jones.

And yet his own Templeton World Fund grew so fast in 1981–1982 that it was almost equal in size to his original fund, World being about $801 million; Growth, about $841 million.

In general, the type of advice close to Templeton's heart combines hardheaded financial common sense with the strong spiritual values he has always prided himself on: "See ye first the Kingdom of God and His righteousness, and make a resolution to save 50 cents out of every dollar."

4
James Dines

In 1960 a young securities analyst named James Dines, working at the time as a newsletter writer for A. M. Kidder & Company, was going through some musty old chart books when he noticed an interesting and seemingly inexplicable movement of certain stock market trends. He was focusing on the years 1928, 1929, and 1930, trying to puzzle out reasons for the market crash of 1929.

It was easy enough to trace all the stock prices and to find that almost all of them in 1929 had gone down, down, and down. All of them as well had been high before the fall, heading up. The turning point in 1929 had simply reversed the long rise to the peak and transformed it into a long decline into the 1930s.

However, not all stocks had performed in exactly the same manner simultaneously. Contrary to the trend, certain issues were moving on an upward curve. Dines was perplexed. He made more studies, checked his figures and calculations, and found that indeed his first impressions were correct. And, what was more, all the stocks that were moving in an opposite direction to the mass were of one specific type.

They were all gold mining stocks.

For example, Alaska Juneau Goldmines moved from 1 to 25 when almost everything else was heading the other way. Homestake, another gold mining stock, multiplied tenfold in a short time.

From that discovery, Dines predicated his Dines Rules of Gold Countercyclicity, "which," he once admitted, "is a real mouthful."

Although he never committed the entire rule to paper, he once described its rudiments: "The rule says that gold and stock prices will move opposite *generally*, but not with mathematical precision."

Dines held that in a time of inflation the value of gold would automatically assert itself by being stronger in the long run than the value of the paper money and the shares of companies traded on the various stock markets. Even though the U.S. government was on the gold standard all through the 1920s, there was so much credit extension that the value of each dollar bill was dramatically decreased.

At the time Dines made his discovery, the country was in a period of prosperity, with the Dow Jones Industrial Average moving on an upward sweep that had begun during World War II and would continue for a few years after 1960. However, he was suspicious of government policy. He felt that the public was being kidded about the strength of the dollar; that the inflated dollar was worth much less than the average person was aware.

Furthermore, he believed even then that there was a distinct possibility that the dollar might have to be devalued once again in the same way it had been devalued during the Great Depression. Dines considered Roosevelt's move to raise the price of gold from $20.67 to $35 as a devaluation to make up for the inflation of the dollar during the 1920s, when its value against the gold bullion that backed it remained unchanged. He thought that in the 1930s the dollar's worth was so low that it couldn't be used to buy much of anything—however, the economy was so sluggish that prices were unable to rise to their proper level.

When the dollar was stabilized in a position closer to reality—that is, when FDR declared it to be worth $35 an ounce—it was actually stronger in relation to gold than other currencies were.

By that time, most of the world was involved deeply in the Depression. The move failed to stimulate the economy or to help other countries trade with the U.S.

What bothered Dines about Roosevelt's action was the fact that he made it illegal for the public to own gold. Dines thought it was a position that no government could ethically take: gold was the most natural kind of money—the only natural kind, really.

But that was all in the past. Dines in 1960 was focusing his attention on market indicators, trying to read the stock market's moves. His newsletter reflected his unease about inflation. He thought that the stock market was going to suffer a serious decline, if not a collapse.

At the time, that view was most unorthodox. He predicted that the U.S. dollar would be devalued drastically against the Swiss franc, the strongest of the European currencies, basing his prediction on the fact that the dollar was as overvalued in 1960 as it had been in 1933.

He also said that silver would follow gold into its alienated state—that is, that the silver coins used as money in the United States would be debased along with paper money. For obvious reasons, Dines said, there would be a big rise in the value both of gold and silver—not only the metals themselves, but gold and silver mining stocks.

His pronouncements did not sit well with his bosses. "First they told me that gold was only for filling teeth," Dines recalled. "I've heard that since then from none other than the U.S. Treasury."

Nevertheless, he persisted in warning that the country was heading into an earthshaking monetary crisis: "I said that unless the situation with regard to the inflated dollar were corrected, we would eventually wind up with the worst depression in our history."

The top brass at Kidder were not pleased. "We had a big collision about that," Dines said. "They allowed me to put a small blurb in about gold, but they were generally resistant to my expressing my ideas. Finally, they warned me that if I did continue, I would be fired."

Eventually Dines was fired.

It happened in 1962. By that time he had built up quite a respectable following among his newsletter readers. The company had allowed him to call his publication *The Dines Letter*. When he left Kidder, he began publishing the letter on his own.

"I had predicted the 1962 stock market decline," Dines remembered. "That was just about the time I was terminated at Kidder. It was no time to be out of a job or to be starting in a new business, but that was the way it was. I was a victim of my own accurate prognostications."

James Dines graduated from Oberlin College, after which he became a National Honor Scholar and attended the University of Chicago Law School. He was awarded a second law degree at Columbia, then served two years in Korea as a member of Military Intelligence.

When he left the armed services, he went to work for Auerbach, Pollak & Richardson as a junior securities analyst. He didn't even have to ask for the job. As a young law graduate, he had gone to the company to purchase various stocks. The brokers noticed his uncanny accuracy in selecting the right ones, and eventually he was asked how he managed to do it.

Dines replied that he had read some books on technical analysis and had added some of his own rules to the conventional ones. His first successes were in some cases blind luck, but with practice, he began to hit an excellent average. When his brokers at Auerbach, Pollak & Richardson asked him to join them, he obliged, and then gave himself a crash course in technical analysis.

Even from the first, Dines had found his favorite stock. It was American-South African Investment Company, known on the market as ASA. On March 24, 1963, he noted that it was selling at 20⅞. By March 29, it was listed at 33⅞.

But more was happening than ASA's rise. "It is dawning on many people that to defend the dollar," Dines wrote, "*U.S. interest rates will have to go up*; else, money will be transferred from the U.S. to England to take advantage of higher interest rates, and a dollar crisis would ensue. However, *if interest rates go up, this might choke off the boom* in our economy. What a dilemma!" That was written in December 1964.

Obviously, Dines was calling his shots as he saw them; he was completely right about the dilemma eventually to face the country in the 1970s and 1980s.

"Lenin was certainly right," he wrote in October 1965. "There is no subtler, no surer means of overturning the existing basis of society than to debauch the currency. The process engages all the hidden forces of economic law on the side of destruction."

His interest in gold prompted him to take a trip to the Union of South Africa in 1965. He wanted to obtain first-hand information about the country because it contained the largest and richest gold mines in the world.

He interviewed businessmen, political leaders, miners, farmers, and Bantu tribesmen. He visited the South African Stock Exchange, went to see factories of all kinds, and climbed down into gold mines.

What he saw and what he experienced convinced him even more of the worth of gold and of its permanent value. Upon his return to the U.S., he continued to recommend gold stocks as a good hedge against a falling stock market.

In April 1966 Dines predicted a market downturn during the year. "*We still envision a monetary crisis*," he warned his readers. In fact, the Dow dropped from just under 1000 at 994.20 on January 18 to 774.88 on September 8 before it steadied and began to come back. It took three years to reach just below its 1966 peak at 968.85 on April 14, and then once again it plummeted in 1970, this time down into the low 700s.

Although he was right about the market, he was wrong about gold. Gold did not rise as the market sank. In 1971 the dollar was devalued, marking one completely correct call that Dines had made in 1963 in these words: "We counsel you to maintain investment positions in gold stocks to protect against the inevitable devaluation of the dollar, which most authorities vow will never occur."

In 1974 Dines' worries about high interest rates were realized; for the first time in American history, they reached double-digit figures. The government finally admitted that there was a "recession."

As for the Dow's plunge in 1974, Dines called it in January, long before it occurred: "We are being paid to call the shots, and we are looking for an immediate market collapse. A decline to DJI 788 for a new low would convince us we were indeed right, and we would look for a devastating plunge toward the 600 area. We know this sounds radical, and that such moves rarely happen." Dines was right. The Dow immediately dropped to around 800, lingered on a plateau for a time, and then plummeted to 577.60 on December 6, closing out the year with a December high of 616.24.

In the same day's communiqué, Dines was able to write: "The price of gold soared to $130 this week."

In 1975 the government finally declared it legal for U.S. citizens to own gold. Dines called for a soaring escalation of gold prices. However, after reaching $198, gold plunged to $103. There the price wallowed in 1976, to begin a steady rise once again, settling in at $340 an ounce in late 1979.

How had Dines' Countercyclicity of Gold fared during the ups and downs of the stock market after 1966?

Not too well.

In the first market plunge in 1966, Dines was confused when gold did not move upward. "Every bear market has its surprises," he wrote in an October newsletter, "and the one area that puzzles us is the refusal of precious metals in the last few months to wait for market mysteries to clear up. For example, precious metal weakness in the latter half of '65 was contracyclical with the market's final blow-off binge, although it was a puzzle at the time. Nonetheless we are more Fundamentalists than Chartists for these two groups, partially because of the fixed floor underneath prices of these two metals and our bullishness on them has in no measure been diluted."

The same thing happened during the 1969 market drop. Gold did not move in a contrary direction at all.

"It then dawned on us," Dines wrote, "that in both cases there was a severe 'tight money' situation! Tight money means high interest rates, and it becomes increasingly unprofitable to own gold on margin. Speculators who feel the price of gold will rise in, say, three years, will balk at paying 10 percent interest rates because that will be over a 30 percent price. And perhaps they only envision a 20 percent rise in the price of gold. So speculators sell gold, particularly when they want to switch back to stocks after a bear market."

To refine his theory, Dines added a condition to his Countercyclicity of Gold rule: "When interest rates are unusually high, golds will drop with stocks at first but should rise when interest rates next drop, if the bear market for other stocks is still going on."

Once the U.S. went off the gold standard in 1971, things changed, and gold began to behave in the way Dines thought it would. The price rose steadily from around $50 an ounce to over $120 in mid-1973, after it had been cut loose from the dollar. During that rise, which was gradual, the Dow had gone up to a peak of 1036.27 on December 11, 1972, and had topped that at 1047.86 on January 8, 1973. Then the market coasted down again to begin a dramatic plunge almost to 600 by December 1974. In 1973 to 1974 gold did indeed rise, although not steadily; but it was at its peak at the end of 1974 before it turned down for a two-year fall to mid-1976.

That fall proved out Dines' theory. With gold going down, the Dow rose from the end of 1974 to a new peak at the end of 1976, when it hit 1014.79 on September 21 and 1004.65 on December 31 for the high peaks before the price slid down steadily to 742.72 on March 6, 1978. During the period 1977 to 1978, gold rose steadily to about $180.

Taking into account Dines's postulate that high interest rates tend to dampen gold prices no matter what other conditions prevail, his theory of Countercyclicity of Gold did prove out in the long run.

From the beginning of his career in stock market analysis, Dines had been fascinated by technical considerations in predicting trends. Like most analysts, he thought very little of the fundamentalist approach, and looked on the market as the be-all and the end-all of finance. However, he was well aware that many traders paid more attention to fundamentals than analyses.

What struck Dines as significant was the way Wall Street operated—more by gut instinct than cool reason. That is, he recognized the power of psychology in the vagaries of market trends, and felt it was every bit as important as either technical analysis or fundamental study.

By the time he had been turning out his newsletter for eleven years, he figured that he knew enough about market gyrations to advise people on the way things were going to go. It was time for him to widen his field of participation. He began putting together a distillation of his thoughts and feelings about the stock market.

When he had all these ideas in manuscript—and the assembled material comprised a huge collection of papers—he looked for a publisher. The compilation of all his thoughts and some of his newsletter pieces made such a formidable-appearing tome that he found interest all but nonexistent.

No book publisher would touch it. Dines knew he had a salable book, and so he used his own publishing company—the

Dines Chart Company—and published the volume himself in 1972. It was called *How the Average Investor Can Use Technical Analysis for Stock Profits.*

It was an enormous work, almost as long as its title suggested. Reminiscent of Joseph Granville's tome on technical analysis, it contained 600 pages. Each was full typewriter-size—8½" by 11"—typed in elite type, single spaced. The text ran to almost 400,000 words. The pages were broken up into sections, with cartoon illustrations included to relieve the monotony of the huge blocks of single-spaced type.

The book contained a great deal of interesting and informative material. In his preface, Dines explained his goals. He was aiming at a readership of people who wanted to know more about the market and how it worked. He had written the material so it could be easily understood. He would examine the market from three different aspects: the *psychological*, the *technical*, and the *fundamental*: "We have given short shrift to Fundamental aspects, because that is what most financial books are about. We have given greatest emphasis to Technical Analysis; there are breakthroughs herein which have never appeared in print anywhere else before, and might prompt some controversy. We expect the psychological section will cause some discussion, because this tackles the psychoanalysis of gambling on a Freudian level."

To make his book readable, Dines used the tricks of writing he had perfected in his newsletter. Sections were introduced by clever subtitles. One read: "The Relationship of Sex to Investing." And the text was as bouncy as the subhead: "In print we once read about a speculator boasting, 'We knocked the stock up 10 points.' To 'knock up,' in slang," Dines hastened to explain, "means to impregnate."

Mainly, Dines used the section on psychology to explain the underlying reasons for mass market-rises and falls—the "vibes" that make for pessimism and optimism. He included material on "year-end rallies," a theory that the year ended with the market going up, stories about "the fall fall," and other curious theories such as the unexplained "seasonal movements."

The bulk of the book covered technical analysis, including a large number of theories Dines called his own, such as the Dines Theory of Market Relativity, the Dines Mirror Trick, the Dines Leap Concept, the Dines Covering Process, the Dines Wolf Pack Theory, the Dines Theory of Positive Negativism, the Dines DuPont Indicator, the Dines ⅗.5 A/D Rule, and the Dines Minus 21,000 Rule.

Generally, the section on technical analysis was complete, understandable, and concise. Dines had noticed the same thing about market moves that astute investors such as John Templeton had observed: that the best way to sell was to select a time during a rise when no one else was selling. Dines called this the Theory of Positive Negativism: "If the public emotionally stampedes in one direction or the other on a topic other than provable scientific fact, they will be wrong reliably often enough for you to go safely in the opposite direction." And the theory worked out particularly well in the stock market.

"Keep in mind the Theory of Positive Negativism, being especially alert for stocks either everyone likes or dislikes. When these stocks begin to move in the opposite direction from mass opinion, pay close attention indeed. The biggest profits will come when you acquire the stocks hardest to buy. They will look too high and have little relationship to their true value at these levels, but remember stocks tend to discount in advance what is going to come, and if sharply rising earnings are just ahead then the high-price stock may not be overpriced at all."

Interestingly enough, while Dines admired Granville and his technical astuteness, he thought very little of Ralph Elliott, with his complex system of determining market moves: "We have no intention of even discussing the Elliott Wave Theory, which we find incomprehensible. Most books pretending to reveal Elliott's

secrets have managed to retain them." Dines' principal complaint was that "The main trouble we find is that it tends to work
except when it doesn't."

Dines included a thorough discussion of the Dow Theory,
pointing out at the beginning that Charles Dow had said, "The
great mistake made by the public is paying attention to price
instead of value." John Templeton certainly agreed. Yet Dines
wrote: "The above anti-chartist quotation from Dow suggests
Dow himself would be shocked at how much his work has become a basis for Technical Analysis, not to mention the volumes
of material written about him."

In his material on fundamental analysis, Dines explained how
to differentiate between "underpriced" and "overpriced" stocks,
explaining the price/earnings ratio and other ways to select
growth stocks for good capital gains.

In his discussion on fundamental analysis, Dines included an
interesting opinion on the relationship of unemployment to the
economy. He pointed out that high unemployment usually dis-
couraged investors because it indicated, seemingly, that the
economy was in deep trouble. Such a reaction, he claimed, was
erroneous: "We think when unemployment is high you have a
bullish indication. This is a Technical way of thinking rather
than Fundamental, and reverses the procedures used by most
economists." In that view he disagreed with Dow, one of the first
to equate unemployment with lower stock quotations.

The book was well received by Dines' fellow analysts on Wall
Street. John C. Boland at *Barron's* called it a "superb book on
technical analysis." Later, Dines commented on the book itself,
saying that it was based more on short-term technical analysis
than on longer-term trends. In fact, by the late 1970s he had
revised his impression of the Elliott Wave and had become a
believer. "At the time I wrote that book, I barely understood [the
Wave Theory]," he explained.

In mid-1973 Dines was writing in his newsletter: "This is a

bear market of unknown depth, length or cause." And he added: "Keep buying gold shares." He was right on both counts; the market was headed down and gold was headed up to a new high in 1975.

As the stock market continued to sink, Dines predicted a "massive bust," accompanied by a falling market of "unknown depth." The Dow didn't hit the bottom he predicted. In the spring of 1975 it recovered, moving from just over 600 to a high of 1014.79 in September 1976. Then it sank again into the 900s. By the time the recovery became evident, Dines once again predicted a depression by the end of the 1970s.

But, he kept saying, because the stock market was going down, the price of gold would go up. He was wrong. His obsession with gold was blinkering him. Gold continued to drop steadily from a peak of about $180 an ounce in 1975 to about $100 in mid-1976; then it reversed and began a steady climb back—up and up and up.

In spite of his inaccurate gold calls, Dines was making astute stock market analyses. In October 1974 he said that the Dow, at that time in the 600s, was about to start a major upsurge. It quite rightly did, zooming in 1975 to a peak of 878.99 on June 30, then tapering off, but continuing to rise in January 1976 to 975.28 and finally reaching 1004.65 on December 30, 1976, even though it had hit 1014.79 in September.

With the Dow at 907 in January 1976, Dines issued what he called "half a buy signal." At that point, the Dow had already finished three-quarters of its twenty-one-month rise from 577.60 to 1014.79. Most of his followers felt that he should have issued his call earlier. But at least he eventually came out with the proper prediction.

One call Dines did make was the big move upward in the price of stocks in blue jeans during the blue-jean siege of America. However, when the market fell apart two years later, he was caught short with his sell recommendations.

All in all, 1975 was a good year for Dines. He was still on

target with most of his predictions, and he had finally managed to collate more of his material to put it in the form of a second book. *The Invisible Crash* was much broader in scope than his first book on technical analysis.

He composed it in a different form because he wanted to reach the people who read his newsletter, and he knew these people wanted advice on the stock market without going into the difficult rudiments of analysis. In addition, Dines wanted to propound his own financial-political theories. He had never kept them secret from his newsletter subscribers. He wanted to influence readers to make the right choice in the politicians they elected, which in turn, he thought, would make for a better country.

Dines sold his second book to Random House, largely on the strength of the success of his first. *The Invisible Crash* had a subtitle: *What It Is, Why It Happened, How to Protect Yourself Against It.* The book was, in effect, a conventional doomsday book predicting depression and chaos.

"America could awake one anguished morning to find itself close to bankruptcy," he wrote, more or less outlining his thesis. "It will have happened slowly, yet its end will be swift. This book will tell you what you can do to protect yourself during the coming crisis."

The book jacket didn't call Dines the Original Goldbug, as he might have preferred, but said that he had been scoffed at as a "prophet of gloom and doom."

His style closely paralleled that of his newsletter—hard-hitting, terse, and theatrical. He opened one chapter: "*How Did We Get Here:* A Devastating Historical Exposé. The real economic history which inexorably led us to the Crash of 1929, and which could lead us to much worse ahead: Not to be found in economics textbooks."

Actually, the chapter was nothing more than a review of coin debasement in early history. He laid the fall of Greece, Rome, and the Eastern Roman Empire to this cause.

Dines was known as the Original Goldbug for good reason. Essentially, his theory was that the only money worth anything was gold or silver; any substitute metal or substitute paper was false and deceitful because it allowed the government (king, prime minister, president, or dictator) to manipulate its value.

Exploring the phenomenon of inflation—the end result of coin debasement—Dines then got to the root of his investment theory. He traced the financial history of the United States, which had begun with a currency based on the gold standard, and continued his narrative into the twentieth century. He showed that there were financial ups and downs, but no single great disaster until the 1930s, when FDR debased the currency. Then, when the country turned from a policy of little government to one of big government, with spending substituted for saving and easy money substituted for hard money, the trouble began.

"In other words," Dines wrote, "we are suffering from a cumulation of all the mistakes since the New Deal." That pretty well summed up his approach. He called the OPEC crisis a logical result of inflationary trends: "The Arabs no longer trust paper. The jig is up, Keynesians. It is the end of the economic 'system' we now have."

Elaborating on the debacle he saw coming, he pointed out: "Food riots and a devastating stock market decline could be fueled by the unrest sparked by unemployment. As I have pointed out, the only way to stop unemployment without a police state is by a free market."

Seven years before government officials began discussing the so-called "flat tax plan," by which everyone would pay a certain percentage of income to the government regardless of his or her income, Dines was considering his own "Dines Tax Plan."

"Here's the skeleton of my tax plan, whereby a new money could be printed once a year with, for example, 10 percent more paper money printed. . . . The government takes that extra percentage for its needs, and nobody pays more than a 10 percent tax. . . . There are no 'deductions' for anyone, so all special interest lobbyists can leave Washington. Everybody in the country would pay an equal, fair tax, including the Church, farmers, the Mafia, and even oil men."

In general, Dines blamed America's ills, including the flight of the middle class to the suburbs, the inability of Detroit to compete in world markets, and the degeneration of quality workmanship on inflation. He put the blame for economic insolvency on the move by the government in 1971 to go off the gold standard: "The action taken that fateful day in 1971 will continue to be a major destabilizing political force throughout Western civilization, and the problems will not be solved until a blatant economic smash shatters the complacency and drives from office the people who got us there."

But there was a way out: To go after gold and silver stocks, particularly Anglo-American. "All the Way With ASA," became a rallying cry for his followers.

Reaction to the book was predictable. It was ignored by the regular book reviewing media but commented on in financial journals. Since many of the people in finance tended to be hard-money investors, they were more or less in sympathy with Dines' arguments—except of course the hysteria they considered a "head for the hills, boys!" syndrome.

An *Esquire* editor interviewed Dines for a front-of-the-book piece. "James Dines, perennial market bear and one of America's most famous goldbugs," he reported, "is alive, well, and living in Belvedere, California."

Noting that Dines seemed even more cynical than in the past, the editor said that the theme of Dines' discussion was "The country's going to the dogs."

"Dines, you may recall," the piece continued, "used to publish his newsletter from offices in New York. But he left the Big Apple for California in late 1976 amid reports that his investment

advisory business had turned sour because of his steadfastly bullish posture on gold during its sharp and lengthy decline in price
(from nearly $200 an ounce to about $100)."

Intimating that Dines was cadging a meal at *Esquire*'s expense,
the writer went on to describe the goldbug's enormous appetite:
"After dinner, Dines, occasionally scribbling with a gold-plated
pen, and, at one point, expounding his gold theories to a bosomy
blond sitting nearby, reemphasized for the twenty-ninth time that
the U.S. is in very bad shape. It was the familiar time-worn
Dines theme: 'We're headed for a cataclysm . . . the Dow Jones
Industrials are going below four hundred . . . a financial collapse
is coming and many banks will fail . . . we're in for depression
and no one will escape . . . gold (which he expects will top $250
an ounce by year's end) is our salvation. . . .'"

And: "Democracy is finished; the communists or fascists will
take us all over.

"If you want to be first, people will think you're crazy," Dines
told the editor, "and you'll have to accept that. But you wait,
someday there'll be economic chaos . . . nobody will escape it
. . . and then I'll have my credibility."

"It was then," the report concluded, "you'll pardon me, that I
started to . . . z-z-z-z-."

Nevertheless, in spite of criticism, Dines continued to dispense
advice through his newsletter, making some good calls and some
bad ones. The broad success of his second book opened up the
lecture circuit to him. He began appearing on talk shows. More
and more magazines and newspapers were running stories about
him and his newsletter.

His image as a promoter of gold stocks gave him a great deal of
press coverage. He had dubbed himself the Original Goldbug in
his newsletter. The term was taken up by the media, and Dines
appeared on the cover of a financial magazine, with antennae
sticking out of the top of his head.

Nineteen seventy-four was the goldbug year to remember. "You had a lot of speculative buying," Dines later told a *Barron's* interviewer. "People buying on heavy margin, who knocked gold down so hard. The more it knocked it down, the more margin calls it triggered."

By 1978 Dines was somewhat doubtful about gold: "My story is still regarded with pessimism and skepticism, as it has been since gold was $35. It's when the majority agrees with me that I'll know we're very close to a top. The public is not into gold right now. They're not interested. The number of gold ads you see now are minuscule compared with what happened at the '74 top or what will appear in the final top of gold."

As for the stock market, Dines gave a sell signal on August 17, 1978. He had issued a buy signal in June. "You have to keep the short, intermediate and long-term very carefully separate here," he explained. "On a super cycle, late '68 saw the beginning of a major bear market, which I said would end below 400 on the Dow. That's still my view, absolutely unchanged. On the inter-mediate wave, there was a buy at 768 in March. It wasn't the exact bottom, but I got pretty close to it. And that's still on as far as I'm concerned, we're in an intermediate upturn. Since then, there have been several short-term buys and sells. . . . I'm look-ing for a rise to about 900."

Supercycles? Intermediate waves?

"I am making my Super-Cycle prediction based on the Elliott Wave and others."

In December 1978, with the Dow at 814.97, Dines said that gambling stocks would help lead the market up toward 900. He was right about them, but wrong about secondary stocks, which made good money for their buyers. Dines simply ignored them.

As for the Dow, it did not reach 900 in 1979 at all; it was February 13, 1980, before the market broke 900, standing at 903.84 on February 13.

By then, Dines had decided that the market was acting much

too erratically for him to predict individual stocks anymore. He said that the market was now strictly for the speculators and warned his followers not to become involved in any buying and selling.

His readings of the Elliott Wave, he said, told him that there was only trouble ahead for the Dow.

As for the Elliott Wave, and what it meant . . .

In 1938 a retired accountant named Ralph N. Elliott was trying to concoct a foolproof formula by which he could mathematically analyze stock market trends far more precisely than by Charles H. Dow's familiar method.

Elliott plotted the various moves up and down, measured their length and duration, and computed the extent of the trends. Then he went back and analyzed the up-and-down waves, trying to find any hidden "signals" in previous moves that would predict the eventual market moves.

He felt that the general waves of the price index were much too vague; he wanted more concise patterns. By measuring each move more accurately, he thought he might uncover some esoteric signals that could be used as new indicators.

His precise graph of the Dow Jones Industrial Averages over a period of years tried to uncover telltale foreshadowings of future directions: "It's a system of recognizing patterns of formation in market averages," one of his followers explained, "from which you can deduce the next likely move in the market."

However, there was much more to Elliott's Wave Theory, as he finally named it, than the wrinkles in the Dow's ups and downs. It proved beyond a doubt what had been thought for many years: that the stock market moved in reaction to the psychology of the investors who bought stocks and bonds. And that mass psychology in turn reacted to and fed on itself in a swelling pattern known as the Fibonacci Ratio.

Before going into the Fibonacci Ratio, the key element in the

Elliott Wave Theory, it is necessary to trace further the intricate patterns that Elliott used in breaking down the DJIA tracings.

Ultimately, Elliott discovered that the market moved in a series of waves—with the number 5 a key consideration—over a period of months and years. But these large waves were only part of the theory.

He refined his five waves by dividing them into smaller ones, called "impulse waves." These he divided once again into wavelets. Each of the three upward waves, Waves 1, 3, and 5, he divided into five wavelets apiece. Each of the two downward waves, Waves 2 and 4, he divided into three wavelets, down, up, and down again.

In addition to these divisions and subdivisions, Elliott named his various types of waves the Grand Supercycle, Supercycle, Primary, Intermediate, Minor, and so on.

He also devised various other methods of breaking up his wave lines by intersecting them with other lines drawn across them as opposite forces acting on the main "impulse" forces. These opposite forces he called "legs."

Thus, in an upward trend of the market, the pattern of the waves had three legs, moving in the direction of the trend (up). These in turn were interspersed with two legs moving against the trend (down). The bull-market configuration showed three up legs and two down ones. The bear-market configuration showed two up legs and three down ones.

And, of course, working against the impulse waves were other waves, called "counter waves." These had two legs going against the dominant trend, interspersed with one leg following the trend.

The waves were found to move in a pattern that, as has been mentioned, resembled the Fibonacci Ratio. When the market was rising slightly, there was a reaction when people who had made a profit sold out. The selling caused the market to turn down for a bit, forming Wave 2. When prices got lower, bargain hunters bought in and the market once again rose with the increase in buying. This time Wave 3 was a bit higher than the previous wave. The rise in turn stimulated profit takers to sell, causing the market to turn down once again for Wave 4 to a point somewhat lower than the first bottom (Wave 2). The reason the move went down further was the fact that the weight of mass psychology *pushed* it down further; thus, the market was really reacting on itself.

In turn, Wave 5, which started when bargain hunters once again shopped for stocks, was higher than Wave 4; the next bottom was lower, and so on. However, that was only half the story. The biggest swing was reached in Wave 5; then the conformation was over.

Now, getting back to the Fibonacci Ratio. Elliott had been working on his graphs for some time before he discovered that the waves he was constructing ultimately broke down into lengths and angles that resembled a configuration dating back to the Fibonacci Ratio, discovered in the thirteenth century.

It was then that the Italian mathematician first identified a number of sequences in which each number was the sum of the previous two. That is, in a sequence beginning with 1, the sequence would be 1, 1, 2, 3, 5, 8, . . . (1 plus 1 is 2, 1 plus 2 is 3, 2 plus 3 is 5, 3 plus 5 is 8, . . .)

Each number, with the exception of the first two, Fibonacci discovered, was equal to .618 of the number following it. That is, 2 divided by .618 was 3.2362 (rounded off to 3), 3 divided by .618 was 4.85436 (rounded off to 5), 5 divided by .618 was 8.0906 (rounded off to 8), and so on.

And 1 divided by .618 was 1.618! It was the only decimal whose inverse (the digit 1 divided by the decimal) equaled the sum of the decimal plus 1.

Fibonacci discovered that there were more magical properties to his ratio. By studying measurements of the Great Pyramid of Giza, he discovered that the same ratio existed in the structure.

Thus, in those days when magic was considered part of science, the ratio became the magic number.

Fibonacci's Ratio was exactly the same as the artist's Golden Rectangle—the ratio of width to length that was decided to be the most pleasing to the eye. Its rule stated that the ratio of the width to the length should be equal to the ratio of the length to the sum of width and length.

Note that the typical numbers used in the Golden Rectangle would be 3 units by 5 units. That is, 3 is to 5 as 5 is to 8, with the 8 actually 8.33 rounded off to 8. In the number sequence, the 4th, 5th, and 6th numbers are 3, 5, and 8.

When Elliott discovered that the angles and wave lengths of his system echoed the Fibonacci Wave, he knew that he was onto an important discovery. And then, in studying his figures, he realized to his surprise that the legs in each of these crucial configurations bore a Fibonacci relationship to one another.

It was a statistician's dream come true—not to mention that of an artist.

All stock market trends could be explained by Elliott's "impulse" and "corrective" waves. In turn, to hone down to precise figures the actual movements, each wave had a subwave and each subwave had a smaller, minisubwave. The largest wave of the configuration was called the "Grand Supercycle," and the smallest wave of all was the "Sub-minette."

Analysis of the stock market by means of the Elliott Wave depended on the computations of the theorist using the wave. One of James Dines' competitors, Robert Prechter, based an entire theory of buying and selling on the wave, even calling his newsletter *The Elliott Wave Theorist*.

According to Prechter, in 1979 all signs pointed up for the market. He thought that the Dow was on the third leg of a primary wave heading upward. That would mean that it would go up to 1200 in 1980, when the fifth wave began pushing up. And that it would be at 2860 by 1983–1984. That figure, 2860, would represent the Supercycle's top, after which there would be a slide to perhaps 300.

Richard Russell, another of Dines' competitors and publisher of *The Dow Theory Letter*, also used the Elliott Wave in his computations. But his considerations saw the market already in 1979 at the beginning of the "fifth and final bull wave." Once that wave was over, he predicted, "The debt buildup in the country will be so substantial that a crash will be inevitable."

By the end of the 1970s, Dines had become enchanted by the Elliott Wave and its ability to predict stock market moves. His computations showed that the wave was working fine; the only differences he had with Prechter and Russell were that the market was not on the fifth wave or the third wave at all. "The bull market ended in 1966 at 1000." What he meant was that 1966 saw the Grand Supercycle; everything ahead was downhill. All he saw ahead was "massacre."

"We're in a supercycle major bear market," he said in 1978. "All advances will be temporary. There will be no new bull market. There will be no run to 1900 or 2000 or 3000 on the Dow; that will not happen yet. We first have to complete the bear market, which has been pushed off by monetary authorities time and again since 1968 by printing more paper money. I think the world is in a very serious economic pause here, and I think it's the final stage of the plateau."

He had been bullish in 1972 and 1973, but as he later explained, "only short-term."

"I think we'll have a drop and then a rally. That rally should end this intermediate up wave, and we should then move to what I call the killer wave. I've been talking about it for years. And I still predict that we'll see it within the next few years. When it comes, it will put the Dow below 400."

The "killer wave" Dines referred to in late 1979 was of course the beginning of the huge bear market that would wipe out everyone. Well, not *quite* everyone.

"The function of a bear market is to restore property to its rightful owners," he conceded. "As this bear market proceeds, it will clean out all the debt excesses since 1932. We've been building these things into the system—the 1946 Unemployment Act, all the other legislation—all that's going to have to go through a purge."

Dines based his assumption on the market drop squarely on the performance of gold: "Gold made a new all-time high [in 1979]. It might be a funny prediction, but I mean it as a serious one. If gold is signaling a major new advance here, then we are close. It's not mathematically precise, but when gold went above its 1974 high, it suggested that the DJIA would likewise go below its 1974 low. My other studies show that for the moment this market is in an uptrend."

And there were more evidences of disaster in the air: "There are things beginning to happen that show me we are not too far away, such as the dollar's collapse overseas and high interest rates. But I don't know when it will be."

Dines had perfected his technique of forecasting. For short-term predictions, he and his staff of technicians used 201 technical indicators to make their prognostications. He called the composite of these indicators, and his eventual forecast, the Dines Prescience Index. He favored what he called the du Pont Indicator in his computations.

"Du Pont tends to move ahead of the market. It's a very good indicator."

In addition, Dines used his Gold Countercyclicity Rule: "When the relative strength of gold is stronger than the market, then it's bearish for the market; and vice versa, it's bullish for the market."

Along with his two prime indicators, he also used Gould's Daily Trading Barometer: "That's a moving average of the Dow volume, issues traded, and also advances and declines. I use moving averages a lot. I use an enormous amount of odd-lot work. When odd-lot short-selling gets under 1,000 shares, we are near a very serious peak."

Edson Gould had developed his Daily Trading Barometer for *Barron's* in February 1970; he was a personal friend of Dines', and Dines thought very highly of him and his system.

In late 1979 Dines noticed that the market was experiencing day after day of short-selling under 1,000 shares. That indicated to him that the market was near a big break. Either that or the rule was no longer valid because of options trading. "You can't get a precise thing out of odd-lot figures," he admitted.

"I expect a very strong rally in the fourth quarter that'll turn everybody bullish for 1979. And then I'm looking for a very bad bear market, the killer wave, to start sometime next year. We'll see what happens."

What really happened was quite different. He issued a buy signal in November 1979, when the Dow was at 800.68. Then, on January 16, 1980, when the Dow was at 865.19, he sent out a sell signal. Instead of dropping, the market continued up. Within a month, the Dow had risen to 903.84, reaching that point on February 13. In his February 15 letter Dines told his followers that he had probably "been early" in his instructions to sell.

In April 1980 he amended his apology to insist that "Our January sell signal was certainly a TDL [The Dines Letter] bull's-eye."

However, the bear market Dines had been expecting again failed to materialize, and on April 9 he issued a buy signal. The Dow was at 785.92. Instead of rising, the Dow continued to fall, to 759.13, where it finally bottomed out on April 21. That left Dines' followers a bit disconcerted, holding the bag as the market sank down past them while they held stocks shrinking in value.

Dines did not issue a sell order. Although he was still anticipating a big drop, he couldn't really promise it. He had acted shrewdly by holding fast. By July 25 the market was up again at 918.43. Somehow, the Elliott Curve had betrayed him. Still, Dines' instincts told him that the market was going to drop once again. He could sit still no longer. He issued a sell order to his people to get out of everything.

Consternation.

The market continued to rise. "That was a little early," he admitted, referring to his sell order, "but I took good profits. I could have called the top a little closer, but most stocks made their highs in August and September. I don't need to catch every penny on every move."

The market moved up at least 100 points after his sell signal, then declined the same 100 points all over again, and then once again advanced another 100. It was acting like a yo-yo. Other advisers were using these moves to make money for their clients. Dines held fast.

"It's not how close you call the market turns that counts," he said, "but whether you make money for your clients."

In 1980 Dines was mostly concerned about "gigantic bull traps" and "graveyards in the sky." In other words, he was warning off his followers. His predictions in 1980 were based on the firm belief that "the major bull market begun in July 1932, ended 34 years later." He said that he was placing his reputation on the line in predicting that a major bear market began at 1001.11 on February 2, 1966.

That particular bear market, he said, "tricked most investors into remaining long-term optimistic for an incredible 15 years." He went on: "Since then, TDL has been warning that advances above 1000 were entering what we baptized 'The DJI's Graveyard in the Sky,' and indeed it looks as if this will be our greatest prediction ever."

Dines was looking for "the Second Great Depression" in the early 1980s. "It is vital that you remain calm, collected and constructive under pressure, and instead of panic, carefully plan precautions."

The precautions were investments in gold and silver mining stocks and in Treasury bills.

In July 1979 the New York attorney general alleged that the Dines portfolio listing gold and silver stocks and their perfor- mances was not in accord with his newsletter claims. Dines' information, mailed out to prospective subscribers, contained "discrepancies," the charge stated. The attorney general said that the portfolio showing that anyone who followed Dines' advice would have made 11 percent on his or her money was incorrect. They would have lost 6 percent.

The complaint also stated that Dines' firm, which published the newsletter, had a capital deficit of $163,026 that wasn't men- tioned in the pitch letter. Nor did the pitch letter say that the model portfolio had produced the 6 percent loss—$6,209.

When Dines refused to accept the attorney general's figures, he was temporarily barred from dispensing financial advice in New York state.

"I'm indignant," Dines told a *Fortune* reporter. "My portfolio made money. It was the attorney general who made a mistake in arithmetic—a negligent [negligible] error of computation." The difference, however, was substantial.

The August hearing was postponed. Nothing happened for some months. Finally, in March 1981, the attorney general's office dropped their suit against *The Dines Letter* and lifted the injunction against him. He was once more free to dispense ad- vice and counsel in New York state.

In early 1980 the handwriting was on the wall. The goldbug industry was facing a rough future. The metal boomed tremen- dously and then collapsed resoundingly. Its days of $400 an ounce were far in the past, and by 1982 it was floundering around the low or middle $300s. Dines might well have waited; by March 1983 it was $450 again, and on the rise. However, he did not wait.

Even in November 1980, Dines was hinting that he was readying his famous "golden bullet"—his call that had been threatening for a long time—his "Much Vaunted All Out One and Only Gold and Silver Sell Signal," which he called and pronounced "MVAOOAOGASSS."

"I'll take one clean shot, hit or miss!" he promised. He then told the faithful that the golden bullet call was no longer far in the future. It was almost here.

When gold boomed and slumped, Dines hedged a bit. The sell signal "will come when it comes." He was taking a lesson from Yogi Berra, whose comment as the Yankees continued losing the crucial game was: "It ain't over till it's over."

In late 1979 Dines joined a New York City company called China Trade Corporation as special assistant to the chairman and chief executive officer. He was hired to try to find new partners to do business with the Chinese.

"The winds of change are blowing across China," Dines said in a *Fortune* story. "I want to encourage American business to get into China on the ground floor."

As for his former title of the Original Goldbug: "I've already won the grand prix and the heavyweight title in gold. I'm looking for new challenges!"

Fortune described him as "a master of the telling cliché."

China Trade's subsidiaries marketed Chinese vodka and beer, conducted seminars on China, organized film festivals, and involved themselves in other activities. Dines immediately set out for China, visiting other areas in the Far East as well: Tokyo, Kyoto, Shanghai, Canton, and Hong Kong.

His itinerary was reminiscent of his earlier travels in South Africa, when he had set out to learn all he could about gold mine values first-hand.

"I want to spend as much time in the Orient as I can," he said. He began preparing a "Dines Model Asian Portfolio" to replace his time-worn portfolio of precious metals stocks. In the early months of 1981 he cut back the publication of his newsletter from two issues a month to one.

"I will be more bitterly criticized for selling out at the top than I was for buying at the bottom," Dines noted wryly.

Some of his first efforts for China Trade were in marketing leather and selling road-building equipment to China, the cost to be shared jointly by U.S. industry and the Chinese government.

Meanwhile gold—to which Dines had first hitched his star— had risen to $875 an ounce during the first months of 1980 and then plummeted to below $550, rallying to $750 during the summer months, falling to $600 by the end of the year, and dropping to just above $400 in the summer of 1981. After a slight rise toward the end of 1981 to the $500 level, it once again sank and was about $350 during the first months of 1982.

It was, of course, nowhere near the hoped-for $2,000 that Dines had once predicted. But he held back from giving his sell call on gold; he still wanted to help his followers get out of the metal at its peak. Two peaks had passed in 1980 without any word from Dines.

In 1982, with the stock market slumping after its over-1000 moves in 1981, wavering desultorily between 875 and 800 during the first half of 1982, Dines was becoming more and more unhappy about gold's inability to perform according to its peculiar qualities: that is, to rise during times of distress.

In the words of one gold researcher, 1981 had been "a particularly frustrating one for gold's true believers. With virtually every major financial and fixed-income market ending the year with a loss, and with geopolitical developments continuing to deteriorate, goldbugs had good reason to expect some better reward for their loyalty."

For their pains, they experienced an unexpected drubbing in March 1982, when gold dropped to $320 an ounce—the lowest price in two and a half years.

What was going wrong? Traditionally, as Dines and other analysts had always maintained, money flowed into gold in times of international stress. The assassination of Anwar Sadat had caused a slight rise, and so had the declaration of martial law in Poland, but there was no sustained rise.

There were at least two reasons for gold's unusual behavior. Russia had been forced to raise foreign cash to pay off enormous bank debts run up following the Polish crisis; she had also unloaded gold to raise money to buy grain purchases to compensate for a very bad 1981 harvest.

"If it were not for the very heavy Russian sales, gold would probably be $100 an ounce higher," gold experts believed.

By now Dines was studying the charts with as much pessimism as he had ever viewed them. For once he agreed that the future for gold did not look good at all. It was time for him to bite the golden bullet.

And so, reluctantly and with a heavy heart, Dines finally sent telegrams to his faithful subscribers, telling them to sell their gold holdings. It was June 16, 1982.

"We decided to sell all precious metals in model portfolios," he wrote.

Even to those who did not follow Dines, it was the end of a very special epoch in finance—the Goldbug Era.

"It's like the Pope just said to everybody, you should all become Episcopalians," commented James Sinclair, a fellow goldbug who had told his followers to bail out in August 1980.

Dines' telegrams were heeded. On Thursday, June 17, 1982, following receipt of the wires, hundreds of goldbugs unloaded their bullion. The price of gold cracked the bottom barriers that had held since September 1979, dropping to $304 an ounce.

Not all Wall Streeters believed that the unprecedented drop in gold prices—and silver prices— was a result of Dines' MVAOOCOGASSS. It was, some claimed, high interest rates and the resultant effect on the U.S. dollar that were responsible. However, they had to admit that the Dines telegram had added to the pressure.

For Dines, it was a mournful and conclusive move. He had promised to get his followers out of the gold market at its peak; he was some $550 an ounce shy of that goal.

All in all, it was a sad curtain closer for the Original Goldbug.

5
Howard Ruff

It was November 1968 when everything fell apart for Howard Ruff. He was thirty-seven years old and had been running a fairly profitable speed-reading franchise for the Evelyn Wood Reading Dynamics Company. But quite suddenly, in the midst of unprecedented prosperity, the franchise was hit first by declining revenues and then by a citywide newspaper strike in San Francisco that was called during the peak advertising months.

Representatives from the national company sat down with Ruff in his San Francisco office for a hard-nosed confrontation. At the end of the meeting Ruff was out of a job and the business he had been trying to save was finished. He was forced to declare personal bankruptcy. He was broke, with $11.36 in his pocket.

More than that, his bank accounts had been frozen. Because he was an employer and not an employee, he was not eligible for unemployment compensation. There were no likely prospects for a job just then; he hadn't thought he would go out of business or he would have been looking.

News of his business failure hit the financial pages of the Bay Area newspapers, and quite soon Ruff was anathema; the Oakland Symphony Finance Committee, of which he was a member, even took the trouble to invite him to resign. "I was embarrassing them," Ruff reported.

He was embarrassing himself, too. He had experienced a checkered career after dropping out of Brigham Young University, trying for singing jobs, acting in plays, taking a shot at being a stockbroker, and teaching real estate investment. Now, to his chagrin, he found himself in debt to the tune of $250,000.

"I determined to someday repay every debt," he wrote, "even though my legal obligation was discharged through the process of bankruptcy."

He called together his family—he had a wife and nine children—and announced his intention to make it back to the top again.

"I had reached that point in life in which you are either trampled or your learn. My wife, Kay, and I made a calculated decision to rub our noses in the whole mess and learn everything possible about the management of money."

Ruff studied every aspect of the economy from as many different angles as he could in order to understand the mechanics of his failure. He used his skills gained as head of the Evelyn Wood franchise—reading quickly and accurately—and amassed an immense general knowledge of finance and economics, both practical and theoretical.

He assimilated everything he read, correct or incorrect. A pattern seemed to emerge. The country was not in good economic shape. In fact, it seemed quite obvious that there was going to be another crackup resembling the 1929 debacle.

Not everyone agreed. He made no attempt to comment on the economy; what he did was learn all the tricks he could about raising money and running a business. Although many of his friends had turned their backs on him—who wants to be associated with a loser?—he did manage to scrounge up a sum of money with which he launched a vitamin and food supplement distributorship in the Bay Area.

The business didn't start out like a house afire, but within a year or so it was reasonably prosperous.

In addition to the distributorship, Ruff became involved with an acquaintance in a discount diamond dealership. He was surprised at how much money there was in diamonds, and determined to see if he could parlay his success at discounting diamonds into other aspects of business. His principal failure in the speed-reading franchise had been in generating enough income to keep the company going. If raising money indeed proved to be the root of the trouble, he would concentrate more on this.

Ruff was learning things about America and Americans in his two businesses. The Vietnam War, into which the United States had plunged with such intensity during the last months of John F. Kennedy's presidency—"to save Vietnam from Chinese communism"—had turned into a no-win war that almost tore the country in two.

Draft evasion became heroic. Young men fled to Canada and Sweden. The flower children opposed the Establishment's warmaking and "materialistic" attitudes. Survival became a fetish. Survival strategy included backpacks and what went into them—namely, dried food, the kind of thing Ruff was now selling. And it included one more item: diamonds.

Persons with anti-Establishment feelings recalled the flight of the Jews during Hitler's time. Refugees had converted all possessions into diamonds (and gold). Ruff understood the psychology. He had been brought up a Mormon, and the history of that faith was one of alienation and persecution as they fought bitterly to establish a homeland.

What he was seeing and what he was hearing from the people he talked to every day inspired him to write a book. It was called *Famine and Survival in America,* a composite of all the things he had speed-read when he was trying to hit the comeback trail—a hodgepodge of economic theory and political cant.

Some years later, Ruff himself would denigrate the effort as an example of early overkill: "It was a crummy book filled with halfbaked economic theory. I hadn't learned the art of creating just enough alarm to stimulate action, as opposed to sounding like a scream in the night."

Nonetheless, according to one source the book sold 200,000 copies. It is currently difficult to locate; even most libraries don't carry it.

Ruff's meanderings on Mount Parnassus had acquainted him with one magnificent truth about people: most of them were frightened of the future; many feared losing all they owned; most were frightened of inflation, which was eating away the value of their money. One book wasn't the way to stir them up. Constant advice would.

In 1976 Ruff sold his food distributorship to raise money to start a brand new business. He was going to become a publisher.

And so, that year, was born *Ruff Times*—a pun on his name and on the epoch. The weekly communication would give advice on money, investment, and money management—the kinds of things Ruff hadn't had when he needed them. He was determined that no one else would have to suffer the way he had.

Howard J. Ruff was born in 1931 in Berkeley, California, the son of devout Mormon parents. His father died when he was an infant, and his mother supported him as a seamstress during the Great Depression years. Although he grew up in the Depression, he was not adversely affected by it. In some ways, living in times of poverty and want taught him to be self-sufficient and independent.

His religious code was fundamentally Mormon, which stressed the Judeo-Christian virtues. He absorbed sound principles of ethics, morality, and economics, and determined early in life never to deviate from them. His mother saw to it that he learned the value of money and understood its power. One of her legacies was the lesson that his personal amount of the world's wealth was a "stewardship" and that he had a responsibility to protect it and to magnify it.

Although many Christians made the mistake of believing that money is the root of all evil, Ruff was taught early on that this was false: the real lesson was that *love* of money is the root of all evil. The point was that he should understand money and treat it with respect.

After his schooling in Berkeley, Ruff went to Salt Lake City, to Brigham Young University. Up to that time he had never proved to be a particularly brilliant student or even one who seemed aimed in any special academic direction. He was a quick study, but he didn't know quite what he wanted to do.

Personable, good-looking, and charismatic even at that young age, Ruff had developed a remarkably good singing voice during his high school years, once his timbre had settled down. For that reason he majored in music at Brigham Young. He was interested in opera, and studied it with interest. During his vacations he got a job singing in the chorus of the San Francisco Opera.

Because he had to minor in something, he chose economics. It was one of those "snap" courses that everyone took. "I picked my economics minor out of the air," he said later. "By senior year I had run out of money, and got out of college before it did me any personal harm, like ending up teaching high-school music courses."

After dropping out, he joined the Air Force. There he went where his strength was and became a member of the "Singing Sergeants." The program director liked his voice so much he made him official announcer for the group as well as featured singer.

When Ruff was discharged, he looked around for work, again in the musical field. There were both singing and acting jobs to be had. It wasn't hard for him to audition and win a part. He had stage presence, a good memory, and the ability to charm those about him. One of his favorite occupations was playing in Gilbert and Sullivan's light operas. During this period he sang on the *Ed Sullivan Hour* and the *Colgate Comedy Hour.*

Show business proved to be much too unstable for him. He married in the 1950s and began his family, which eventually would include nine children. Tiring of a grueling life that seemed to mostly involve running around looking for work, he entered a brand-new phase of his life when he went to work for a stockbroker in San Francisco.

The stock market fascinated him almost immediately. He had a healthy respect for money, and he soon realized that it exerted a powerful influence on anyone who came near it. He became a broker and did moderately well. He began to realize how political maneuvering affects the financial world in monumental ways, and came to mistrust the government and its inability to keep its hands off business.

Ruff was restless for other fields to conquer. He went on the road as a salesman. He pushed food supplements at first, then switched to cosmetics, cleaning products, and freeze-dried foods.

"I didn't jump on fads and abandon them," he said. "I accumulated them. I guess you could accuse Michelangelo of jumping on a lot of fads, too, whatever they'd pay him to do."

In spite of his presumption, Ruff was no Michelangelo.

He was pushing weight-loss programs at one point, then tired of the routine and decided to settle down in a small business of his own. There was an Evelyn Wood Reading Dynamics franchise up for grabs in San Francisco; Ruff interviewed for it, raised the money to buy in, and became the sole proprietor.

By now he had been around enough to know most of the ropes in the business world. He had benefited from a course given by one of the teachers sent out from the national headquaters. The speed-reading business was in full swing in the nation at the time, and Ruff was signing up people in droves.

But the 1960s were divisive times, particularly in the San Francisco area. Although all the kooks and crackpots were not confined to that part of the country, the Vietnam backlash and the hippie frontlash split the community wide open.

The verities—education, hard work, family life, devotion to

duty—became relics of the past. The Establishment lay bleeding in the streets.

Along with the Establishment went Ruff's franchise, which was facing troubled times because many of the college students who would have been taking the course were either dying in Vietnam or evading the draft somewhere. The cash flow dried up. Ruff found it difficult to meet his office bills, much less make payments to national headquarters.

And then his franchise was canceled and he went into bankruptcy, as has already been explained.

"I went into work a moderately prosperous man and came out bankrupt. Ruined my whole day," he joked later.

In 1975 an IBM regional marketing representative named John Terry Jeffers called on Ruff in San Francisco, pitching IBM machines. At the time Ruff was the author of a book and was running both a dehydrated-food and a diamond business. The two men struck up a friendship.

"First time I met Howard," Jeffers recalled, "I thought he was way out. But one of the things I saw was that he was a great performer. And what good's a message if no one understands it? I said, 'Howard, you're an incredible product.'"

Ruff laughed. But Jeffers recognized a strength in Ruff that even Ruff didn't understand. When Ruff began talking about his business of supplying Californians with natural foods so they could survive the coming collapse of civilization, Jeffers' eyes opened wide. He thought Ruff was teasing him.

After the mind-boggling 1960s, the country had more or less settled down into the dreary 1970s—all except California. Out there, the kooks and crackpots continued to thrive. But now they weren't trying to save the whales or spike the soldiers, they were trying to figure out how to weather the coming apocalypse. Many of them thought it was already at hand.

"You're too good to be peddling dried apricots and wrinkled prunes," Jeffers told Ruff. "You're a natural!"

A natural what? Ruff wondered.

Jeffers told him. "A natural prophet. If those people are all afraid of what's going to happen—afraid enough to stock up their basements with dried peaches—you're going to help them survive!"

Ruff said quietly that he himself kept an eighteen-month supply of food on hand at all times. It was simply a Mormon type of thing to do. Jeffers was a Mormon himself. He nodded his head. He knew.

Without explicitly saying that they were going to lead their fellow man out of hell and into the promised land, Ruff and Jeffers put together a program that looked very much as if that was what they were trying to do.

Jeffers quit his job with IBM and Ruff sold his dried fruit business. They pooled their money and formed their own publishing company: Target, Inc.

Target's main venture was publishing *Ruff Times*. The newsletter followed in concept Ruff's book, although it certainly went beyond money management. It told people everything Ruff decided they should be told. It was a friendly bit of weekly chitchat.

All the things Ruff had learned when he went on his crash program in economics and money management found their way into its pages. But Jeffers was intelligent enough to realize that Ruff was more performer than prophet. Therefore, he kept Ruff on the right path, performing in print every week for his audience. Occasionally a bit of economic advice slipped in.

Ruff told everyone out there who wanted to hear how he had managed to survive over the years in spite of the hazards and pitfalls of life; if they listened to him he could help.

From the beginning, he took his lead from James Dines and other members of the doom-and-gloom school who had been preaching for years that the economy was going to collapse and that the only thing that could rescue America was a return to the gold standard.

Ruff was no hypocrite, and thoroughly believed in what the

goldbugs were saying. He thought it was a mistake to inflate the
dollar, that Johnson had erred in his guns and butter economy.
He made it his theme.

There was one problem. There weren't enough goldbugs to
support publication of the newsletter. They would have to appeal
to a larger segment of the public. Ruff and Jeffers finally decided
that the key to their approach would be an "enlightened" one that
didn't hew too heavily to the gold-or-nothing syndrome.

Shortly after Target started its weekly newsletter, the message
was more or less established: *The country is caught in a rampant
inflationary cycle. If uncorrected, this inflation could lead to cata-
clysmic social, political and economic chaos.*

The method Ruff used was an ancient one. Like any skilled
preacher, he mesmerized a small, worried flock, preached them
a little fire and brimstone, and then promised to show them the
way out of their trouble to their salvation.

While Ruff was concentrating on the message, Jeffers was
looking at the numbers. He knew enough about publishing and
circulation to realize that a newsletter with 15,000 circulation
was a big winner. Jeffers wanted that and plenty more. He sought
it by using a time-tested hard-sell technique.

By writing direct-mail solicitations that were as fetching and as
enticing as Ruff's newsletter itself, Jeffers managed to build circulation from 0 to 80,000 in three years. He did it by mailing out
over a quarter of a million solicitations the first year, covering
everyone he could possibly get on a mailing list. Five years later
he was sending out from 25 to 30 million letters annually; by
then the circulation was up to 142,000.

Meanwhile, Ruff's message was coalescing into something rich
and strange. In the weekly four-, six-, or eight-pager, he pontifi-
cated on subjects as varied as the price of gold and how to be a
good father when you traveled a lot. His style was that of the
chatty, friendly, streetcorner philosopher.

In order to keep his readers from falling asleep, he underlined

significant words and phrases in almost every sentence. He became extremely personal, discussing his home life, his Mormon-
ism, and what he had been doing with his wife and children.

During the first years, he conceded: "Some people say that I
couldn't succeed at anything—so I became a prophet of doom!"

When he began Target in 1975, Ruff still had a debt of
$175,000 from the Evelyn Wood fiasco. Between 1968 and 1975
he had paid back about $75,000 of the original $250,000 from
the businesses. Now, voluntarily—since he was not required by
law to pay off the $175,000—he erased the debt from his person
and was free and clear for the first time since 1968.

In 1977 Ruff and Jeffers went into partnership with Neal Lar-
son and Paul Galbraith in the Reliance diamond company.
Within a month, Ruff had sold his interest, and Jeffers left six
months later. At the time of the formation of Reliance, Galbraith, who wound up with 50 percent of Reliance, owned 15
percent of Target; he sold that in 1978.

That same year Ruff and Jeffers held a "convention on financial survival," drawing numbers of his faithful readers plus others
interested in understanding the economic roller coaster. By that
time his name had begun to circulate along the lecture circuit,
and soon he was making regular appearances behind the podium.
In 1978 his second annual survival convention drew 5,200 faces
to Anaheim, California.

Meanwhile he had begun producing a half-hour syndicated
television talk show, called *Ruff House*, in which he interviewed
economic and financial pundits. The show was carried on forty-
eight stations by 1979, then on sixty stations covering 300 cities.

Jeffers and Ruff were elated by the early success of *Ruff Times*.
But it seemed to Jeffers that there was still room to expand. The
two partners decided on how to exploit what they already had:
they would write a book more or less carrying the message that

Ruff was giving out every week in *Ruff Times*, but not the one that had dominated his first book.

"It started out as a mail-order text for new subscribers," Ruff said later, referring to the birth of his second book, *How to Prosper During the Coming Bad Years*. "Thirty-five to 40 percent of the book was a cut-and-paste job." Ruff dictated the rest. The book, fed into a word processor, was completed in three months.

Although Ruff was practiced enough now to be able to speak directly to his subscribers, he was too much a ham not to inflict most of his ideas and jokes on his family.

"I run it through my teen-age kids," he said. "And I think I have a knack for making the complex clear."

From the beginning, *How to Prosper* was a winner. Jeffers and Ruff approached seven publishers while the work was in progress, pitching the contents. Out of the seven, six made them offers right away. Because there was such widespread interest—obviously created by the Ruff and Jeffers ploy of leaking the information—Target held a bidding session.

"An interesting bidding war ensued," Ruff said. Eventually, he signed a contract with New York Times Books, and in 1979 the book finally appeared. Almost immediately it was obvious that it was going to encounter what its author called a "deafening silence" from the media.

Slowly it began to receive attention. On April 23, 1979, Ruff's name and picture appeared in *Time*. A profile on him appeared in *The New York Times Book Review* on May 6. (After all, the book *was* a Times Book.) Also in May, he was sneered at by *The Wall Street Journal*, and in October *Money* published a small biography.

As books go, it was exactly in the proper mold. The short chapters were broken up with clever "graphic" subheads, styled with the same flair evident in *Ruff Times*: "Now You See It, Now You Don't"; "Cracks in the Plaster"; "And Now the Bad News."

The major theses had already appeared in his newsletter:

• There is going to be a bad crackup in the United States economy;

• The best thing to do is to move out of the city and buy a house in a small town;

• Be sure to store up a year's supply of food wherever you are; stay away from canned and frozen foods; get dried foods or freeze-dried; guard it, with weapons, if necessary;

• Buy a bag of silver coins for every member of your family in case of a collapse of paper money;

• Get your money out of savings accounts, insurance policies, and investments with a fixed return;

• Buy only things that are important to your survival: house, food, clothes;

• If possible, do not borrow money; pay off all outstanding debts;

• Learn to grow your own food, mend your own clothes, repair your own house.

The book was also a plea for more stability in the economy, although Ruff not for one moment believed it would occur.

"Nineteen seventy-nine and 1980 is a watershed period," he wrote. "Great fortunes are made when rapid economic changes occur, in either direction. Although everybody likes the upturns, equally great opportunities to make money can be grasped by those who catch the downswings and know what to do, even if it's only to avoid the fate of the unaware who will be wiped out."

Inflation was a pet bugaboo with Ruff, just as it was for Dines. After exploring a history of coinage debasement beginning with Diocletian, he described the horrendous inflation in Germany after World War I, and wound up with Will Rogers' sardonic advice: "Invest in inflation, it's the only thing that's going up."

After demolishing the stock and bond markets, he pointed out how Social Security would never work, calling it a "Ponzi Chain Letter."

He blamed the quick and dramatic decline of the South Bronx in New York after World War II on the political expediency of rent controls and welfare. But that rot was not confined to the South Bronx.

"There's not a single city in the United States with over a million population which will not be in financial distress to some degree or another by 1980," he wrote. "All the big cities are in decline."

He then advised his readers to pull up stakes in the big city and buy a place in a small town. He explained that he had done it himself after he discovered that his home in Berkeley was appreciating at a rate of 15 to 25 percent a year—too fast for comfort.

"I picked a small town in the Central Valley of California which is surrounded by a diversified agricultural economy and concluded that it would be one of the beneficiaries of the middle-class exodus from the cities described in the previous chapter. I bought a home and settled down to stay."

Ruff surveyed the banking situation and forecast dire ruin. The whole system was creaking and could go broke any minute. "The best bet is just to avoid banks except for necessary transactions so you won't have to worry about it."

He was particularly upset to learn that the President already had a secret plan to take over all the banks and other lending institutions in case of big economic trouble. "You should have your money out of those areas which are essentially government controlled," Ruff advised, "and I'm referring to banks, the stock market, even the commodities market, at the first sign of trouble."

Mostly Ruff reflected his strict Mormon upbringing in his views of the sociological scene. He saw the family in complete breakdown, morality gone, and authority in ruins. Such a collapse of discipline would lead to apocalypse. He quoted Professor

Urie Bronfenbrenner: "As soon as the family fell apart in Greece and Rome, so did the whole society."

He also described the money market funds and called them a good way to use high interest rates to make money.

Not all reaction to the book was negative. Wall Streeters had already heard all about the end of the world from James Dines, for one, and from staid middle-of-the-roaders like Eliot Janeway. What bothered some of them about Ruff's book was its eloquence.

"It is no secret," wrote Alfred L. Malabre, Jr., of *The Wall Street Journal*, "whether you are writing a book or feeding a daily newspaper, that sex and fear serve to draw in readers. Those of us who labor in the vineyards of financial journalism have considerable difficulty slipping the former into our copy. . . . We are left, accordingly, with fear. Imagine the attention that would be paid this article, for example, had it started off something like this: 'The next depression is likely to begin within two months, and it will make 1929 look like a garden party.'"

But, Malabre went on, he couldn't begin his article that way; all he could do was sit back and nurse his envy at Ruff's ability to stir up such a pother.

"Our envy-level, in fact, took a nasty little jump just the other morning," Malabre wrote. "The flareup came at precisely 8:31 the other Sunday when, as is our custom, we scanned the best-seller list of *The New York Times Book Review* and noted that a book titled *How to Prosper During the Coming Bad Years* was solidly in the number-four spot on the nonfiction list.

"It is, in truth, a pretty awful book."

Malabre pointed out that 35 to 40 percent of it was a cut-and-paste job; he had heard Ruff admit the fact to an interviewer. He noted that most of the material was similar to the doomsday warnings ground out by the Chicken Little-criers like Harry Browne and Harry Schultz. He didn't mention Dines.

After taking Ruff to task for advising everyone to move out of the city, Malabre wound up with: "Sitting in our centrally located New York apartment, we wondered whether the Ruffs had stocked up on gasoline as well as food (of which they have an 18 months' supply). We hoped they had, but flipping through the book we couldn't find that precaution mentioned."

Among the people outraged by the book was "Adam Smith," in actuality investment counselor George J. W. Goodman. A historian of finance, he had written his own fair share of books. His weren't the doom-and-gloom type; even so they were bestsellers just like Ruff's.

Writing about Ruff, Harry Browne, Douglas R. Casey, and Jerome F. Smith, a silver and platinum bug, Adam Smith/Goodman intimated that their success had been preordained by heavy promotion and the bold headlines of their publishers. To him, they were all the "financial version of born-again preaching." They offered damnation—"You will lose everything"—and then redemption—"You are saved if you read this."

About the doom-and-gloom authors, he wrote: "They are well outside any conventional establishment; that is, they have no other calling, they do not profess at universities, nor bank among bankers; their business is advice, specifically advice in the profitable newsletter that each of them publishes."

Smith/Goodman pointed out that Ruff and his ilk were by no means alone in their thinking. The prime rate had hit a record 21 percent, and two years previously the dollar had plunged some 30 percent against certain other currencies before it rallied. OPEC was a survival threat to the oil-consuming states, and the Iran hostages showed the United States' inability to protect its citizens.

But Smith/Goodman did have a bone to pick with the Cassandras:

"My quarrel with the prophets is not with their scare headlines; there are, indeed, several possible crises and we do not need the prophets to run scared. Nor is it necessarily with their personal prescriptions; gold and silver are volatile commodities, nimble traders will make profits, and I hope their Swiss banks are better run than the one I used.

"My quarrel is with their limited vision. Their villains are so easy. We had little inflation in the 1950's and early 1960's; is the current crop of politicians so much more venal? Does 15 percent inflation lead automatically to the wheelbarrow full of money? Alas, our problems are more than mechanical; even balanced budgets and a brake on printing money will not solve energy imbalances, the instability of poor countries, the strains on the banking system, and the presence in the world of real adversaries. Yet we also have a rich, diverse and talented nation, which could mobilize for those tasks. No hint of that."

The book brought more than comments and reviews. It helped establish Ruff as a credible figure—something his newsletter had failed to do. One dehydrated-food distributor in California was most happy with the book and its popularity: its dismal philosophy was selling his product.

"Anything that scares people is good for us," he said, gleefully noting that his nine-year-old firm's annual sales volume would exceed $5 million in 1979. "At first," he said, "we sold mostly to campers and Mormons—Mormons believe in laying away food for hard times, you know. Now they're mostly to people referred to us by Howard."

Another man to profit by Ruff's book was an architect who specialized in "survival homes"—ones that had multiple-fuel heating systems, a lot of storage space, and numerous security features.

"I'm even adding plans for a moderately priced survival home," he said. "That'll be a companion to the costly custom-built model that I now sell to wealthy people with 'special' security needs."

A builder in the Midwest was reluctant to talk about his plans for the future: "I've done a few things," he told a financial reporter, "like put away some food, but I haven't gone overboard. Heck, I believe in America. It's just that I want to play it safe. If I don't have to eat the food I've put away, I can always give it to the Salvation Army."

There were even "Ruff Times" parties. Reminiscent of the "rent parties" held in Harlem during the Great Depression, held to raise money to pay the landlord, ten subscribers to *Ruff Times* met at a Chicago apartment to compare notes on the relative merits of various types of canned and dehydrated foods. In addition, they swapped opinions on investments and discussed why they favored preparation for very hard times.

"I remember the Depression of the 1930s," said a former teacher married to a retired engineer. "My father lost everything, and we all suffered terribly. I had to drop out of college. We had to sell our beautiful home and crowd into a small apartment. Some of the time we didn't have enough to eat. I never want to go through that again."

A young lawyer had no faith in the political system. "It doesn't matter whether the Republicans or Democrats are in—they all adopt the kind of inflationary programs that are ruining the country." He had no hopes for the 1980 election: "That will just decide who will be the captain of the *Titanic*."

A retiree, a former optometrist, compared his survival tactics to buying insurance. "People insure themselves in case their house burns down or they get in an auto accident, don't they? Well, my survival precautions are in my insurance against a depression, and I think that's a lot more likely to happen than my house burning down."

What bothered Ruff was the criticism of various investment counselors that he had no academic credentials in finance: "Look," he protested. "The so-called experts helped bring us chronic inflation and runaway taxes. I'm a guy with a wife, nine kids and a mortgage, trying to beat inflation plus a little.

"The basis of my thinking is the free-market economics of

scholars such as Ludwig Von Mises and the Nobel laureate Friedrich Hayek. Their theories show what caused evils like inflation, recession and shortages. I use their theories to make practical decisions for the average guy who wants to protect his savings."

Ruff denied that he was a negative person: "I get tired of being called a professional pessimist. I spend half my time arguing with the Right that the end is *not* near. But the most important thing in my life is passing on good values to my children, and I'm morally distressed that the financial establishment has found me to be teaching them to be speculators."

He was also concerned about public reaction to his views on inflation: "You know, I think many people have a misconception about the true meaning of the word inflation. Inflation means the money is going broke. It went broke 15 percent last year, because that was the inflation rate. Inflation is *not* rising prices—inflation is shrinking money."

Too many people were losing purchasing power without the vaguest notion how to cut down on their losses: "With the unprecedented changes in our nation's economy in the past decade, we have had to discard the rules we played by in the fifties and the sixties. If you continue to do today what has been considered safe and prudent in the past, you will be losing money over the years, instead of gaining, because of this monster known as inflation—a vicious, evil tax that takes away your purchasing power and slowly renders your money less and less valuable."

The way to combat that loss was to try to purchase investments that provided a good return and still kept ahead of the inflation rate.

Critics accused him of ingoring the obvious way out of the muddle: putting money in Switzerland or other foreign money havens and retiring there.

For them, Ruff had a proper answer: "If America goes to hell, you know the rest of the world will be disaster. I believe the smartest thing is to invest in the long-term future of America while preparing for short-term troubles. That's what the Arabs, Swiss, Japanese and West Germans are doing."

He began picking up big names on his subscription list to *Ruff Times* on the strength of the success of his book. Senators Mike Gravel of Alaska, later killed in a plane crash, and Orrin Hatch of Utah, subscribed, along with actors Lorne Greene and Chuck Conners, Ronald Reagan, Howard Jarvis, and Joseph Coors of Coors beer.

In critiquing Ruff's position on buying gold or silver coins and selling off part of the hoard each year, Patricia A. Dreyfus wrote in *Money*: "This would have paid off, on average, during the past five years, but there were long stretches when it would have meant taking a loss. During those same periods, many bonds were yielding a steady 8 percent to 12 percent, comfortably higher than the inflation rate. Bond interest is taxable as ordinary income, however, while profits on coin deals count as capital gains."

She continued: "Another oversight: the price performance of gold and silver has been anything but stable. In every year from 1973 through 1976 you could have lost 26 percent to 34 percent by having to sell at the wrong time. Ruff says that these 'small losses' are a modest price to pay to 'panic proof' your life. The real force behind Ruff's argument is that most investors can remember a stock that burned them while gold and silver have not yet suffered a prolonged bear market."

That was just about to happen—but not until after one of the most exciting roller-coaster rides up and up and up in history took place.

Toward the end of 1979, Ruff was a happy man. His book had been a runaway best-seller for most of that year—it sold over 450,000 copies. He had sold the paperback rights for $350,000 to Warner Books. His newsletter was taking off again, stimulated by interest in his book. Subscriptions eventually rose to an amazing 160,000.

His television show, *Ruff House*, was syndicated in 275 cities, and he was still appearing everywhere he could on the lecture and talk-show circuit. He was still bullish about gold.

But suddenly, in late 1979, he changed his mind about gold. There was something a bit odd about the usually vigorous metal. It was, to him, a time for a tough decision to be made: "It was the most agonizing [one] . . . in the four-year life of *Ruff Times*. I came to the conclusion that gold, which was reasonably related to such fundamentals as inflation, war and a falling dollar, had become the captive of wild-eyed get-rich-quick amateur speculators. I haven't rejected gold by any means. I've rejected the markets as they're behaving now."

And so he began to warn people not to buy: "The market has turned into a wild gambler's emotional crap-shoot." He switched his policy almost completely, underlining his 180-degree turnaround by advising his followers to buy bonds! For true goldbugs, the bond market was the end of the road: all kinds of paper were hateful to them, and bonds were the worst of all.

Ruff was adamant: "I just think interest rates are likely to come down during the next eighteen months." He prepared himself for disgruntled subscribers to cancel, and had visions of losing some $200,000. He lost a lot, but he didn't take a real beating.

What happened was that he turned out to be right in anticipating a move in gold—and wrong about the direction. Gold, then selling at about $375, skyrocketed at the beginning of 1980. But it was a boom-and-bust situation, not a solid, continuing rise. The price went up to about $875 before it tumbled. Silver hit $50 before it collapsed. Ruff's advice helped some of his subscribers; at least those who believed him. They may have missed the ride up, but they also missed the long journey back down.

However, in January 1980, Ruff decided that they should buy

back their survival coins. By doing so, they would be paying $475 an ounce for what they had sold at $375.

After that he settled down. In April 1980 gold was again around $450. Ruff predicted that it would shoot up to $850 within weeks and then drop to $400. Gold went to $720 in September 1980 and then began to fall again. Ruff told his subscribers to sell in December. The price was in the low $600s. He was right. By July 1981 it was down to almost $400.

Analyzing Ruff's reactions and the accuracy of his predictions, two prestigious financial publications came to opposite conclusions.

One called him "shrewd." John Merwin wrote in *Forbes*: "Ruff's advice, which proved premature, may have cost less nimble readers profits on the way to $850 gold and $50 silver, but it also saved an equal number of amateurs some horrendous losses when the metals crashed back to earth a few weeks later."

Another said his advice in 1979 was bad. A. F. Ehrbar in *Fortune* wrote: "His worst call came on September 20, 1979, when he told readers to dump gold—even their hold-'em-forever survival coins—because the market had turned into 'a wild gambler's emotional crapshoot.'"

In his reversal of policy, Ruff was right about bonds. In the spring of 1980 they rose sharply.

Except for gold, 1980 was a good year for Ruff. He was branching out in all directions in an attempt to increase his income. He suspected that the days of gold fever were coming to an end.

He began putting more and more pressure on his seminar meetings, which paid off very well at about $100 a head. And he even dabbled a bit in politics. In April he formed Ruff PAC to support Senator Steve Symms of Idaho, spending about $116,000 trying to reelect him. He also founded Free the Eagle, a lobbying organization that published a monthly broadside called *Howard J. Ruff's State of the Nation*.

He put together two conventions for 1980 and also a number of seminars. Each engagement brought in $10,000 in fees; they also gave his newsletter beautiful exposure. One seminar took place in San Diego—an annual *Ruff Times* convention—drawing 4,500 followers from all over the nation. A few weeks later he was in Palm Springs, playing to an audience of 200, each of whom paid a premium $1,200 to see him.

Some weeks later he was in Manhattan. He caused some concern among his flock in not showing up for the first day of a two-day show. He apologized; he was behind schedule in writing his forthcoming book, a sequel to his best-seller.

Covering the show were numerous journalists from the New York area, many of them quite wise in the ways of the financial world. One of them commented on the fact that Ruff surprised the audience more than the other speakers did; he dispensed very conventional advice. It was a typical money-management seminar.

Some of the proposals hinted a bit at tax evasion—one was a plan to dodge capital gains taxes due on the sale of a home by asking for the payment in silver coins—but most of the comments were the same old thing.

One person in the audience had come to hear a South African gold specialist and not Ruff.

A housewife complained about his emphasis on passing money on to an heir tax-free: "I want to find out how to get it in the first place!"

A member of a Midwestern coin-brokerage firm took the podium and suggested that everyone invest in precious coins. However, instead of giving the coins away to irresponsible bankers, or even putting them in a safe deposit box, he told them he had a better way to put his money in trust. He said that his collection was in a deep hole in his backyard.

"I took a post augur and went clear to the handle!" he told them. That broke up the crowd.

Ruff was careful never to speak too long at his seminars. He enlivened his appearances with one-liners and theatrical tricks. He held a seminar in China and one on a Caribbean cruise.

He even promoted a special Christmas catalog, with gifts galore. Selections included everyday items such as a telephone bug detector, a $95 home medical kit, a vacuum food packer, and kits for identifying counterfeit gold coins.

He began to sell specially struck *Ruff Times* silver coins and a game called "Life Is Ruff."

In New Orleans, Ruff was present at a conference of the National Committee for Monetary Reform, and it was there he met Tom Bethell, the Washington editor of *Harper's* Magazine. Bethell was interested in Ruff's thoughts on gold. Ruff was expansive: "I could have worked for Carter's reelection and bought gold on margin," he joked, then hastened to add that he hadn't done it. He said he knew that four more years of Carter in 1980 would have sent gold soaring. Reagan had just been elected. Ruff said he was "hopeful" because of the election, but only "mildly so."

"Optimism doesn't come easily to goldbugs," Bethell noted.

Ruff went on: "The political constituencies will remain the same, and there will be more welfare bums like Chrysler. People will turn on Reagan if they don't get what he promised."

Ruff predicted that the price of gold would be "$2,000 or possibly $3,000 by 1983."

Bethell wrote: "He changed his mind on the subject in the few minutes I was with him. He thus managed to embody the confusion of the conference, in the course of which many gurus spoke in diverse tongues. But the prevailing opinion seemed to be: Hold on to your gold—just in case things get worse."

Ruff had predicted trouble, and times were indeed hard for the goldbugs after 1979. After gold's unprecedented rise to $875, it never again remotely neared that figure except for a jump from $550 to $750 in 1980. Then it was on its way down again.

What about those people who had followed the advice of the goldbugs—like Ruff—and put a great deal of their money into gold?

"This is batten-down-the-hatches time," Ruff said. "Guys who haven't diversified their base are being badly hurt."

Tim Metz, a reporter for *The Wall Street Journal*, commented on the decline of gold: "It comes at a time when at least a partial return to the gold standard for currency is being seriously considered by some monetary authorities. What torpedoed the gold price, it appears, had less to do with the usefulness of gold than with its overpromotion. Commodities generally, precious stones, art and other collectibles have suffered from the same hype in the last year."

But the men who had been touting gold were in for a bad year in 1981. One of the country's most revered hard-money groups, the American Economic Council, had lost a great deal of money in 1980 and 1981 when it sponsored its usual annual seminar. Few signed up. In 1981 they wired Ruff to forget about the council.

"I'm afraid they're finished in the business," Ruff said. He had been scheduled as a speaker. "They called up to tell me they weren't going to be able to pay my fees or travel expenses."

Ruff refused to back out, even though they offered to let him cancel his appearance. He went. Out of the 800 to 1,000 expected, only 375 attendees came.

In 1981 Ruff's newsletter began to lose subscriptions. The publication had a usual renewal rate of about 95 percent. Now the dropout rate rose from 5 to 10 or 11 percent.

Ruff also decided to drop his television show. "I just got tired of doing it," he said. "Tired of the talking-heads format and tired of seeing it relegated to fringe-time slots and not taken seriously."

He was becoming increasingly unhappy about his gold stance. "There are hard times for newsletter writers," he admitted in an interview. Indeed they were. High interest rates and the expectation that price rises would moderate had taken the edge off gold as the true inflation hedge.

The professional goldbugs were beginning to jettison their supplies of gold and silver and were telling their followers to do likewise. The obvious alternative to investment in these metals was buying into the growing and prospering money markets. There the average person could achieve returns equal to or even above the inflation rate.

"Mr. Ruff says he hasn't changed his philosophy," Roger Lowenstein wrote in *The Wall Street Journal*, "and that his rigidly no-gold reputation was unjustified. He has said at times that gold was overpriced."

"It's assumed that once you stick the label 'goldbug' on someone he thinks gold can only go up," Ruff said. "If I said that, I'd lose my subscribers."

Although Ruff thought gold would drop below $400 in 1981, he continued to predict that it would hit $2,000 again "in the next major bull move."

It was not the best of times for a hard-money advocate, but then it was not the worst of times either. Ruff had always known that he was sitting on a timebomb in opting to be a soothsayer.

"In this advice business, you don't ever get into it unless you have considerable ego. Otherwise you wouldn't feel that your deathless prose was worth charging for. But what I've added to that ego, which a lot of advisers have, is some pretty heavy marketing skills. You can go out there and get 5,000 people to sign up for your newsletter because there are 5,000 people who will sign up for any hard-money-oriented newsletter. We made a decision to do something other than preach to the already converted. We made a decision to reach beyond them."

He had done so, and he had changed a few lives in the process, many for the better. Still, the whole business sometimes frightened him.

"This nation is ripe to be manipulated by a powerful person-

ality. I am appalled at the ease with which I am acquiring a
following."

In 1981 Ruff wrote and published another book: *Survive &
Win in the Inflationary 80s.* It did very well: in six months
180,000 copies were sold. Ruff was unhappy, however, to find
that it was running at only about half the speed of *Prosper.*

"For me it's an embarrassing flop. I blame that on the current
apathy over gold."

One reviewer found it "oddly comforting" to encounter a
doom-and-gloom book once again, "as if one were sitting down
to reread a Dickens novel filled with one's favorite characters."

But the book wasn't just more of the same. Ruff was changing
some of his ideas. "He has finally betrayed the genre," the critic
continued. "Glimmers of *optimism* are creeping in."

Now Ruff foresaw disaster four to seven years away; in his other
book he had declared ruin was only a year or two down the road.
He spoke in the familiar Ruff style, saying of federal regulators:
"When you have a hammer in your hand, everything looks like a
nail."

In his *Inflationary 80s* book, he abandoned the notion of am-
munition as an exchange medium, but still favored purchasing
gold, bags of silver coins, diamonds, small-town real estate, and
collectibles. He seemed to be moving into the mainstream of
investment, even taking government bonds seriously, particularly
as a counterploy when interest rates and gold declined.

For stocks he had also been experiencing a change of heart: "In
addition to oil, you can also bet that gas, coal, uranium, hydrogen, solar and their related service and equipment industries also
show strong potential for growth in the future."

Investment advice included an aroused interest in the so-called
strategic metals—chromium, cobalt, indium, magnesium, tan-
talum, and tungsten: "Large amounts of 'smart money' are flow-
ing into strategic metals as this is written, and I expect strategic

metals to be the foundation of many fortunes in the decade ahead."

One of Ruff's plans constituted a stroke of genius. He suggested that the government switch the income tax deadline to the Monday before Election Day so that voters would be hot with rage when they reached the polls.

"Politically," one reviewer noted, "he is a libertarian. He thinks conservatives are nearly as big spenders as liberals, without their compassion. His agenda includes fighting regulation, dismantling the federal energy and education departments, returning to the gold standard, and eliminating the capital-gains tax and price ceilings on natural gas."

As for Ruff, he had one personal note to add: "We will press for the deregulation of the newsletter industry by the SEC."

He was still convinced that gold was about to rise again—to at least $1,000. "It will happen when the public realizes that President Reagan can't control inflation. I'm talking a matter of months, not years." He made that statement in September 1981. He was wrong, of course. Gold wallowed in a doldrums, unable to rise from the low 300s, and would sink even lower in 1982.

In looking at Ruff's track record, it is interesting to note that his advice to his subscribers sometimes proved to be better than the advice he gave himself. For example, he started out in the middle 1970s advising his followers to buy gold when it was worth only $120 an ounce. Then he advised selling gold when it hit $425. Early in 1979 he forecast $300 as the top price, and it went far above that. He never readjusted his advice.

His calls have been mixed and have received mixed enthusiasm. The problem of course with someone who predicts future events is that if the prediction is left open-ended, almost anything that happens can count as a plus.

Ruff was right in some of his silver calls, as well as some of his gold calls. He recommended buying $3,000 bags of silver coins, and the value of these coins has about quadrupled. However, his calls on the silver market were equivocal at best.

He was right when he recommended buying diamonds in 1977, long before they reached astronomical figures.

As for small-town real estate, he was right about that too, suggesting that anyone who bought would profit. Real estate, especially in small towns, almost doubled from the time he recommended it. However, urban property probably more than doubled; since he suggested moving out of the cities and into small towns, the owner of a large piece of urban property might have lost on the deal—at least on paper.

As for his own business astuteness, especially when dealing with money, his prescience was sometimes dubious. In 1977 and 1978, when he was trying to finance his newsletter, he issued $1.5 million worth of two-year "gold clause" notes to affluent subscribers. These notes, which were in effect loans, were denominated in both dollars and in the equivalent ounces of gold, priced at the time the notes were issued. The lender had the option of being repaid in cash, bullion, or in bullion value.

When the notes came due two years later, the value of bullion was almost *four times* what it had been at the time the notes were issued. Someone who had lent $50,000 would theoretically be able to collect $200,000!

Obviously Ruff had no way of completely hedging his risk. If he had purchased gold futures, and the price had declined, he would have been stuck with a loss. The much greater risk, of course, would be in a huge increase in the price of gold. Prudence dictated that he hedge with futures. He did—and lost both ways. He took losses on his hedge position when gold fell in 1978, and then was totally unhedged from the beginning of 1979 all the way to December, when gold more than doubled.

When Ruff advised his subscribers to sell their "survival" coins, one observer speculated that he might be trying to drive down the market to minimize his losses on the unhedged notes!

Target apparently lost more than $4 million during those two years. Ruff told *Fortune*, however, that he was unhedged for only a brief period in 1978 when gold rose $55; his total loss, he claimed, was only $455,000.

In late 1980 he again lost by taking his own advice, guessing the wrong way in the futures market. He purchased ten gold and eight silver contracts, when the prices of both were falling rapidly. A gold contract bought 100 ounces; a silver contract, 5,000 ounces. Ruff said he lost only $116,000.

In 1980, when gold was rising, he made up for it by making profits on ASA, a company that invests in South African gold stocks (shades of James Dines!). That profit offset his subsequent losses.

In July 1981 Ruff was once again calling for gold to rise. "I'm thrilled to death that gold has been going down," he wrote. "I feel professionally vindicated, because I've been predicting that gold might go as low as $400 an ounce. Right now I'm cheering for lower, lower, lower. I sent out a buy signal last week at $450. My point for throwing caution to the winds is $400. I'm buying now, and I think the risk-to-reward ratio will be irresistible at $400.

"We could see as low as $375, but that would just give us another marvelous opportunity to buy. Gold will go to $2,000 an ounce sometime in the 1980s; it is possible by the end of 1983. If the next round of inflation hits 25 percent, we'll have $2,000 or $3,000 gold easily."

But so far gold was wallowing badly, making no effort to rise to the heights Ruff was still predicting. Eight months after he wrote his July 1981 predictions, the price was down to $304.

Like most of the hard-money prophets, Ruff was skeptical of the ability of the American economy to shake itself out of its inflationary spiral. If such a turnabout did occur—that is, if inflation were halted and interest rates were turned around— would his doomsday newsletter simply fail?

"If the nation were genuinely confident of its leaders, its policies and its money," Ruff said, "I would be canceled for lack of interest in my *present* message. However, I'm a professional financial adviser. It's my job to help people enhance their capital in good times or bad . . . it really doesn't matter. I'm equally comfortable professionally in either environment."

In 1980 Ruff said: "I'll guarantee you something that will materialize in the next five years. Just when everybody else is saying, 'The end of the world is near, we're about to crash through the bottom, Western civilization is doomed,' my long-term faith in the future of this economy is going to be saying, 'These guys are crazy. Now is the time to make a long-term bet.' We'll be buying up stocks. We'll be doing whatever we have to do. I'll change the name of my newsletter to *Good Times*. I'll change my name if I have to."

In spite of his sanguine comments, he had been taking several steps that would insulate him from any new upturn in the economy and a consequent downturn in the "rough" business. In 1981 he formed New Capital Publications, which publishes newsletters on commodities, real estate, taxes, and stocks. He hired Douglas Casey, author of the best-selling *Crisis Investing*, to write his stock letter. Casey began by recommending penny mining stocks on the Spokane Exchange.

Ruff began looking for other newsletter subjects that wouldn't be hit by slumps in the gold and commodities markets. "We can go with whatever is right for the market at any given time," he said.

In addition to Capital, he started Financial Planning Services, a company that holds seminars around the country and advises professionals and nonprofessionals how to invest. Ruff put his partner, Jeffers, in charge of Financial, with B. Ray Anderson, the writer he hired to do the tax newsletter for Capital, to provide tax and estate-planning savvy.

Example: Raise livestock in the backyard, hire your children to care for them, and thereby transfer your income into a lower bracket.

In addition, Jeffers and some of the other officials of Financial Planning Services formed a company called Newcastle to sell investments to *Ruff Times* subscribers. Ruff made a point of telling his subscribers that he wanted to maintain his credibility by staying out of *that* business.

But he wasn't spending all of his time on financial problems. Late in December 1981, he was busy loosening up his vocal cords for another assault on show business. Then, when no one seemed to be looking, he began recording songs for an album.

"This album was born out of my values, including God, personal integrity, family, American freedom, the American free-enterprise system and responsible financial stewardship."

The original title of the album was to be "Great Songs of Money, Investment, Family Love and Inspiration." But nobody seemed to be breaking down the doors to buy it. The name was then changed to "Songs of Country, Money, Family Love and Inspiration."

Ruff's numbers included, "I Walk Today Where Jesus Walked," "Hymn to America," "If I Were a Rich Man," "Money, Money," "The Impossible Dream," and "Never Walk Alone." He was backed up by the Brigham Young University philharmonic orchestra on several cuts; a choir and some of the Osmonds on others.

In the first months of 1982, Ruff began peddling gold-clause notes. Rumors spread that his motive was a needed infusion of cash to keep his company afloat. Ruff pooh-poohed the idea: he merely needed some working capital to keep his cash flow strong.

In his newsletter, Ruff was expressing a slightly changed posture in relation to gold. He said that the price was not going to change much in the near future. At the same time, he was very bullish, claiming that he planned to buy $450,000 of the gold-clause notes himself, putting them into the company. To finance his operation, he wanted $1 million from his subscribers.

Ruff was counting on inflation to continue, soar, actually. That meant that he was suspicious of Reagan's efforts to cool down inflation and cut back government spending. If Reagan could indeed cripple inflation, it would be a bad blow to Ruff's position as a doom-and-gloom soothsayer, and his money in gold-clause notes would suffer as well.

He insisted that prices would quadruple in the 1980s and that gold would go up to $2,000 an ounce within a few years—echoing the goal earlier stated by James Dines before he reneged and bit the golden bullet.

As for *Ruff Times,* even if Reagan brought down inflation and high prices and cut spending, Ruff thought he had made his publishing empire diversified enough to cover almost any kind of situation that could develop in the economy.

In its early months of operation New Capital Publications soon had a total circulation of 30,000. Things seemed to be coming out of the rough for the resilient Ruff.

But *Ruff Times* was in for its own brand of the same. *Hulbert Financial Digest,* an "investment-letter performance-rating service," rated Ruff's 1981 advice as −2.6 percent. That is, if an investor had followed every one of Ruff's choices during the year, he would have ended up with less money than he had put in at the beginning.

Ruff examined his operation closely. The economy was changing. He decided to extend his own general corporate improvements to his newsletter. The title was a good play on words, but not fitting with the new times. It became *Howard Ruff's Financial Survival Letter.* The idea of survival remained, but the emphasis was less on doomsday panic than on simple financial gain.

With his advisers he prepared a brand-new portfolio. By the end of 1982, Mark Hulbert rated Ruff's newsletter as +33.8. An investor who had followed the publication's advice would have made a one-third profit. The key advance, Hulbert pointed out, was made in December 1982, alone, largely through Ruff's advice to buy one of his old survival favorites—silver!

*   *   *

A *conservative forecaster, a showman turned technician, an astute mutual-fund manager, a goldbug, and a doom-and-gloom soothsayer—these five money messiahs constitute only a small percentage of the thousands of financial advisers in business with newsletters, books, and one-on-one counseling in the stock market.*

In the recent years of inflation, high interest rates, and low stock market quotations, advisers who are called many things—among them "hard-money men," "gold and silver bugs," and "doom-and-gloom-callers"—have amassed a considerable following among retirees living on pensions and persons outside the market generally who want to get in.

Half a dozen or more have made names for themselves by their advice and counsel. Some have written books; others have given advice from lecture platforms; still others have appeared on television talk shows. Among the true hard-money advocates, at least six merit attention.

6
Douglas R. Casey

Based in Washington, D.C., Douglas R. Casey wrote several books, but none did as well as his best-seller, *Crisis Investing*. In a book that made it big even though it was published by the Stratford Press, a relatively small publishing house, Casey made a strong bid for gold as one of the most effective ways to combat government interference in financial affairs: "Gold, as cash, is invisible. That means it is not engraved with serial numbers, or your social security number. If you own it, you are the only one who knows that you own it. This is the most important advantage when it comes to keeping what you have."

It was his contention that a new big depression had already started even at the time he wrote the book (1979). "It's merely a question of how long it will last and how bad it will get. People think we are not a part of history. But we are."

He went on: "The financial collapse is on the way. The standard of living will go down, banks will fail, people who own bonds will be wiped out by 1990. Real estate is the 1929 stock market crash lookalike. It's all borrowed money. Mortgage rates will go higher.

"But people who act sensibly now will do well. They can't live in the past. They can't follow dated prevailing wisdom."

Casey was high on gold even though he knew the depression that was coming would wipe out the world as we know it.

"Stock up on light bulbs, toothpaste, and other basic commodities. Put your serious long-term money in gold, not as a speculation for next year but for five years hence, and in strategic metals, too."

Casey's thesis on inflation paralleled earlier explorations of it by tracing its growth through the debasement of coinage through the ages all the way up to America's shift to devaluation by the President in the 1930s. The twin evils of inflation and abandonment of the gold standard in 1971 caused the economy to go into a tailspin.

Because the economy suffered, so did the stock market. Instead of a slow, steady pace upward, as had occurred in the postwar years since 1945, the pace was accelerated, the dollar went wild, and the European moneymen began to turn in dollars for gold. To forestall a run on the dollar, the U.S. went off the gold standard.

The result, Casey said, was an attempt to ease the strain by price and wage controls. After this failed, the country drifted until the monetarists began to tighten the amount of money in circulation. Dampening inflation from this perspective increased interest rates, causing horrendous problems in the economy generally.

The stock market suffered because the business community was unable to get cheap money to finance new ventures.

"Learn to become a creative and prudent speculator," Casey advised. "This is psychologically difficult for some people, but you must adjust to the 1980s. You must speculate or you will lose your capital."

Casey blamed the unions and business—working in collusion—for causing many of the problems in the economy: "What about Chrysler and other large corporations having their problems? Let them collapse. Let them go back to work producing goods and services that people here and abroad really need. Let them make it in the competitive market place on the basis of their own wisdom, skill, and ingenuity."

In spite of his hard-money theories and his faith in gold and silver, Casey favored investing in the stock market: "To be fair, I do think common stocks have some assets. Certain selective stocks can perform well and provide a good return, but you have to track them very carefully. Bonds have no assets at all."

He never had much faith in the way bureaucracy tried to cut inflation: "The government is going to try to choke the depression to death. It won't work. It never has. What we need is a genuine free market, without all the artificial supports and constraints."

Education, intelligence, and political savvy could be a valuable asset in trying to live within the economic parameters: "It is essential to understand the economic process. Learn what causes inflation. Learn why unemployment rises. Learn why interest rates go up, why banks become vulnerable, why bonds offer no real hope. The people who act wisely now will be the new millionaires, while most others will be wiped out."

7
Harry Schultz

Although he was born in America and lived here most of his life, Harry Schultz moved away to live the expatriate life of a millionaire in Switzerland. Whether or not his exile was prompted by income tax reasons, we don't know, and he rarely if ever appears in the country of his birth to attend seminars or meetings. He sends over taped cassettes of his current financial philosophy recorded in his own voice.

Publisher of *The International Harry Schultz Letter*, he also wrote several books espousing, in general, the same cause: put your money into gold and silver and other solid investments.

Schultz's newsletter appears every three or four weeks, written and spelled in a special language invented by the author to give the reader the idea that he or she is "on the inside" with the movers and shakers.

"At last," one issue started out, "here's the *real* story on how Mugabe won the Rhodesian election & why it surprised everyone. Had it been an *honest* election, Bishop Muzorewa wud probably have won 36seats, Mugabe 24seats & Nkomo 20seats. An hslm [Harry Schultz Letter Man] bizman who lives there gave me this inside story."

The Schultz letter is a combination of specific investment advice and confidential information supposedly gleaned from secret sources, all overlaid with a tinge of right-wing politics: "Arab buying was evident in silver in Sept. Euro mkts only. . . . Grain harvest estimates trimmed (price bulletins) . . . USSR buying coffee . . . *Gold:* gave longterm bull signals. Shorterm is foggy. London fix chart needs 2fixes over 694 to give traders buy cue. . . ."

But the times they were a-changing, and Harry Schultz could see that gold's longtime bull signals were getting weaker and weaker. Through 1981 he wavered, but by 1982 he was convinced that gold as the final solution was in real trouble.

Reasons? Inflation was being brought under control. War now seemed unlikely. The banking crisis around the world seemed to have receded.

And, because of those unexpected developments internationally, Schultz began to worry about the status of his old love. By the end of 1982 he finally broke down and admitted it:

"Gold is in a bear market!"

That was quite a change of heart for the man who had written in 1972: "Hence by buying gold in some form you are in effect freezing your assets at a given value and allowing all other things around you to fluctuate economically, knowing that ultimately no matter how far out of line they have become, things will be measured against gold, sooner or later."

But if gold was no longer the way to go—where was the road to security?

Schultz knew the answer. In December 1982 he was advising his apostles to sell their land, to sell their stocks, to sell their bonds, their metals, and go into cold cash.

Cold cash?

The longtime goldbug had undergone an astounding metamorphosis and emerged as a true 1980s phenomenon—the dollarbug.

8
James E. Sinclair

One investment adviser fixated on metals generally—including gold and silver—is James E. Sinclair, head of the New York commodity and security companies that bear his name. The co-author with Harry D. Schultz of the book *How the Experts Buy and Sell Gold Bullion, Gold Stock, and Gold Coins,* he usually advised investors during the 1970s to purchase gold stocks as well as other types of metal stocks, with his main thrust always in specific metals. He made a great deal of money in precious metals and currency trading during those years—for himself as well as for his clients.

His suggested portfolio has included metals like antimony, chromium, cobalt, germanium, rhodium, titanium, and electro manganese (manganese obtained by electrolysis as opposed to reduction).

"The opportunities in strategic metals exceed opportunities in precious metals, even though the latter are greater," he said then.

In late 1980 Sinclair was mostly concerned about the vulnerability of strategic metals found in places like Africa, and that of course included the most precious of all metals, gold. He announced then that gold was having its greatest day, on the assumption that because of the unrest in Africa it would be difficult to obtain and thus would be more valuable in the future.

He predicted that gold might show strength from 1980 into early 1981, but then would drop. That "chop" might carry prices down to $375. Then investors would have "the last great buying opportunity." Gold would rise once again, so much so that the January 1980 peak at $875 could prove "more a base than a top."

He also pulled for silver to hit $100 an ounce. He based both assumptions on the fact that geopolitical problems were insoluble, making strategic *and* precious metals valuable.

Shortly after he prophesied this, the price of gold dropped and silver wallowed in a trough. Silver was nowhere near $100. It was then that Sinclair did an about-face. "I would advise my customers that the only recovery in gold is cyclical in nature," he said. "The great drama of gold is past. A move from $35 to $887.50 is a once-in-a-lifetime event. If that's what you're looking for, you've missed it."

In a recent interview in 1982, Sinclair said that he was looking into four specific areas to make money during the 1980s. They were Treasury bills, Treasury bonds, stock market index futures, and industrial metals.

Sinclair even admitted that he is not hot at all on gold anymore.

9
Ian McAvity

"I am more impressed by the action that has taken place in gold and currencies than by the potential upside in the New York stock market." So wrote Ian McAvity in the December 1979 issue of *Deliberations*, the newsletter he sends from his Toronto home.

One of the few publishers of newsletters who gives stock market prognostications and also follows the fortunes of gold and the metals as well as currencies, McAvity is known as one of the most knowledgeable of the technical chart writers. He provides a range of useful charts that are almost impossible to find anywhere else. They include advisory sentiment, ten-day moving averages, advance/decline line, and volume.

McAvity never became a goldbug—that is, committed to it in the form of a quasi-religion like his fellow gold-lovers—but he usually seems bullish about its prospects.

He was bearish about the stock market in 1979, and this continued in 1980, in spite of the spectacular 250-point advance. He expected the market to drop, and he stuck by his guns, even though he was wrong.

He was bothered by the inverted yield-curve during the period from October 1978 to May 1980. The "inverted curve" referred to the ratio of short-term interest rates to long-term rates. At the time, short-term interest rates had moved above long-term rates. McAvity knew that such periods always presaged an average drop in the market of nearly 20 percent. The drop occurred some four months after the interest rates had peaked.

All during the summer of 1980 he awaited the correction, missing the move he kept seeing as a bear market rally. By the end of a year in which he had been mostly wrong about the market, he said that "1980's very strong advance must be considered vulnerable to major weakness in the 'postelection' year of 1981."

He based his conclusion on his own postelection year market charts. He looked for a 25 percent fallback in the market. "Then the stage could be set for the DJIA to finally break away from the four-digit phobia, perhaps. But we have to get through 1981 first, and a 'tummy-tester' appears to be imminent."

McAvity was right about the stock market, but wrong about the timing. The market spent 1981 rising just past the 1000 mark several times, but then sliding down into the 850s to close out the year, going down even further in the first half of 1982. And gold continued to fall as well, making its most serious drop in 1982, before coming back in the summer.

10
Harry Browne

From his base of Austin, Texas, Harry Browne had dispensed his own homegrown brand of hard-money advice in his *Harry Browne's Special Reports* newsletter long before he became a best-selling author and guru of the hard-money, hard-metal crowd currently billeted in Zurich.

One of the few newsletter writers who was also a best-selling author on financial topics, Browne had never worked on Wall Street and was a self-made, self-educated man.

From the beginning he courted the "little guy," pointing out to him or her how a fortune could be made in the market without the advice of the financial experts.

His newsletter had always plugged gold as a permanent store of value, unlike paper money. He urged his followers to get into gold and silver from the early 1970s, when gold was $35 an ounce.

He put his money where his mouth was, as the saying goes; while advocating gold, he buried bullion in his backyard. While touting Krugerrands, he lodged them in his safe deposit box. While pushing South African stocks, he bought them from his broker. While lauding silver, he stashed some away in his vault at home.

He came to national attention in 1970 when he first turned his hand to writing full-length material in book form. His first book, *How to Profit from the Coming Devaluation*, appeared just one

year before the generally unexpected devaluation and move off
the gold standard, which he had clearly anticipated.

His prescience was noted; he became a credible figure and
began appearing at hard-money seminars and on television talk
shows. He was right about the devaluation but a bit off the mark
in his assertion that there would be an "economic revolution"
within five years. However, there was a mild recession in 1973.

In 1974 his second book appeared. *You Can Profit from a
Monetary Crisis* became an immediate best-seller, and he became an even more popular figure on the lecture circuit.

With his doom-and-gloom preachments, Browne unequivo-
cally advocated gold, silver, and Swiss francs for their solidity and
greater strength and endurance over the paper dollar.

His advice was not confined to gold: "Trade what you have—
paper money, real estate, and other properties—for silver
coins. . . . Bury them in the safest place you can find."

An investor following Browne's advice could have purchased a
bag of silver coins with a face value of $1,000—worth $3,366 in
1974—and in 1979 its value would have increased to $8,472!

His third book, *New Profits from the Monetary Crisis*,
appeared in 1978. The folksy style of his two earlier works was
replaced by a much weightier tone. This time Browne accurately
forecast an inflation rate of over 10 percent; it occurred the very
next year.

"You can no longer rely upon *any* long-term, buy and hold
investment strategy to take care of you," he wrote. "The swings
between bull and bear markets will be too extreme."

Browne suggested greater flexibility in investments, including
stocks—a new tack. The idea was to divide the investments into
two portfolios, the first to consist of the metals and Swiss francs,
and the second to contain stocks and bonds.

"When the substitute disappears, people turn to the real
thing," Browne explained, referring to paper currency versus
gold.

In 1980 he was living in Europe, and flew in to attend a hard-money seminar in New Orleans. He appeared with bad news about gold: "For me," he said, "the bull market in gold ended in January. Before the next cyclical upswing begins in late 1981 or early 1982, the metal's price can plunge to $400 an ounce." The downtrend would be strengthened by the election of Ronald Reagan.

"It's time to be suspicious of hard money," Browne declared, making his followers jump a bit. "We're not going to make money in the 1980s repeating the investment wisdom of the 1970s. Hard money has become a religious experience. There are people today who buy gold as an act of faith. Gold and silver are becoming icons."

Neither gold, silver, nor the Swiss franc were the unique investments they had been when metals prices were held down by government decree. It was dangerous, he added, to persist too long in any one conventional investment theory. For example, you could no longer rely on the old cliché: "Borrow money and pay it back with cheaper dollars."

So now gold was on the skids? Heresy? Probably. But Browne proved to be right. After the big 1980 boom and bust, gold was through as a glamour acquisition.

11
C. Verne Myers

Described as a "visionary" and "a genuine oracle," C. Verne
Myers was born in Saskatchewan and began his career as a
geologist. He then went into journalism before becoming a guru
of finance. His interest in geology—particularly oil and gas—was
why he called his newsletter, begun in the 1960s, *Myers' Finance
& Energy Letter.*

Myers had started a Canadian oil and gas journal around 1940,
but sold it in the 1960s to begin his financial newsletter. As early
as 1972, he was telling his readers to take their money out of the
stock market and the banks because the market was headed down
and the banks were paying less interest than inflation was taking
away.

"Put your money 100 percent into gold," he said, "and in gold
mining shares." Gold was selling at about $35 an ounce then—at
least it was as soon as it was legal to own it.

In 1975 gold was selling at between $165 and $170 an ounce,
but Myers warned his followers out of it in August and advised
them to put their money into U.S. Treasury notes paying 8 to 10
percent.

Two years later he put them half back in gold, in January, at
$135 an ounce, then fully back in February, at $140 an ounce.
In October 1978, when gold hit $220, he advised his subscribers
to sit tight.

"If you simply *have* to do something, though, the best action you can take is to sell one-third of your gold and invest the proceeds in South African mining stocks."

On March 30, 1979, gold was $241.50. Myers predicted it would go to $1,000. By July 20, with gold at $298.75, he was still sanguine. "This is not a speculative market. It is a huge volcano building steam."

On September 14, with gold at $332.20, Myers said: "This movement is like a tidal wave. The force is so great that the ebbing will be small, while the flow will be steep." On September 27 gold was $395.50. "A 100 percent investment in gold is not a risk at all. It is a retreat into safety."

On October 19—$380.50—Myers was holding. On November 16—$386—Myers was holding. "People are now beginning to hoard greenbacks. The banks are getting shaky." On December 7 gold was $439. "It's only a question of time."

By January 4 gold was $624. And on January 17 it was $800. Eventually it reached $875. Myers was still holding firm. However, when it hit its peak, anyone who had purchased gold when Myers first told them to would have turned $10,000 into $200,000!

In 1975 Myers had published a book, *The Coming Deflation— Its Dangers—And Opportunities*, predicting monetary crisis, currency debacle, energy outage, stock and bond massacre, labor disruption, and food shortages.

By 1979 he had added one more crisis to his original six: war. He correctly predicted a Russian move in the Middle East, not naming Afghanistan, but implying it. "The military implications are huge. The political stakes the most important we have ever faced. The U.S. must arrive on the scene in force. Nothing less than this can secure the safety of the energy supply for the Western World over the next few years."

Well, not quite.

But it was a nice ride for the goldbugs and the hard-money men on the way up.

*   *   *

By the end of 1980, the goldbug movement was pretty much a thing of the past, although of course many followers were still holding on to their bullion and gold stocks.

Interest was beginning to refocus on the stock market, although the Dow was certainly not making a historical break past 1000 to surge on its way to 2000, as some of the faithful had been contending. The financial world was in the doldrums, with high interest rates and inflation eating away at prosperity and causing a laggard economic picture to develop.

Among the most respected and watched of the technical analysts still making a career of Dow-watching there existed a handful of die-hards.

12
Martin Zweig

Probably the most accurate of the forecasters is Martin E. Zweig, whose subscription list of about 5,500 is no barometer of his true stature in the field. A holder of a doctorate in finance, Zweig supplemented his newsletter publication with regular appearances on *Wall Street Week,* the Louis Rukeyser weekly half hour on television's PBS network. In addition to his letter, which makes about twenty appearances a year, Zweig has a special telephone service that adds a twice-a-week phone recording for all his customers as an added feature.

Zweig prides himself on his ability to see trends in the making, but is honest enough to admit that he can't always time his predictions for the maximum benefit of his readers: "I've integrated a lot of momentum indicators into my model, and it's very hard to get out at the exact top or in at the exact bottom with momentum. But I'm willing to pay the price of some whipsaws to stay on the right side of the market. I'm usually going to be a little late."

The letter states exactly what Zweig recommends, with no nebulous loopholes to provide copouts. He makes a distinction between "newer speculations" in stocks and "long positions." His letter advises stops on all stocks; when a stock advances, he usually moves the stops up. Then, when he feels that the market is ready to slow down, he tightens the stops to reduce risks. His handling of predictions is thoroughly conservative and almost defensive: "I don't tell people I'm going to make them millions by getting them in at the bottom and out at the top. I take a more scientific approach to the market. And I try to protect people."

In recent years, Zweig made a perfect call in November 1979 by turning bullish and in doing so hit the February 13, 1980, high of 903.34 right on the nose. And, most expeditiously, he then pulled out of nearly all the stocks in his portfolio, remaining conservative through the April 21 lows, when he began calling for a rise again.

In May 1980 he was "powerfully bullish," his first such feeling in five years. The Dow advanced all through the summer, but Zweig began to hesitate in September. He was right; the market did fall in late September. In October he was buying again. By the middle of December he was going cautious and advising no buying.

At the year's end he was bullish, but in January 1981, less so. The market hit 1000.17 on November 20 and 1004.69 on January 6. By the end of 1981 it was in the 800s once again.

And, in the spring of 1982, all indications were that the trend was bearish instead of bullish. Most advisers were suggesting their investors sell. What is called the "buy-sell" ratios were pointing to another bottoming out.

Zweig was suspicious of these indicators, called "sentiment" indicators by market analysts. "I used to go hogwild over them, but I'm more suspicious now."

In mid-June the market fell to 788 and then rebounded to 812. It went down again, but bounced back. Zweig remained cool, deciding that it would begin up again—but not until after a leisurely wait.

He was right again. But he did not realize how long he was going to have to wait. Early in August he was feeling bearish.

"We might be heading into a depression," he said. He was worried about the falling interest rates. But he hedged. "The odds are three to one against it." Then suddenly he felt the market was in for a change of mood.

It was on August 18, 1982, that he finally gave the buy signal in his newsletter. "Every bull market," he explained later, "begins with a powerful advance in its early weeks. It needs that momentum in order to propel it higher and higher in the months that follow, just as a rocket needs potent thrust to get into orbit."

By October 1982 he felt that the market was in an extremely bullish phase. All the sentiment indicators were signaling an upward movement. It would go, he felt, from 150 to 200 points in four months or so, to 1200.

Zweig was right. It hit and passed 1200 in six months, on April 26, 1983.

When the *Hulbert Financial Digest* analyzed his 1982 year's performance, Mark Hulbert found Martin Zweig's *Zweig Forecast* to have achieved the top performance of the year. According to Hulbert's charts, if an investor had followed all its counsel, he would have made an 80.3 percent gain over the year.

Zweig reformed his newsletter during 1982, making it more and more an electronic response rather than a printed mailer by advising his investors what to do by means of telephone. At a slightly inflated fee, of course.

His feeling is still bullish in today's market situation, with the Dow consistently above 1200.

13
Robert Prechter

The Keeper of the Flame for Ralph N. Elliott turned out to be Robert Prechter, who created a business out of charting the stock market according to the rules and regulations laid down by his mentor when Elliott developed his trend-forecasting method years ago.

Prechter's newsletter, called *The Elliott Wave Theorist*, was created to provide the wave's advocates and believers with an eleven-issue-a-year report on how it sees the Dow's gyrations during the year, and how it predicts coming months.

The publication makes no specific stock recommendations, but simply forecasts the major market trends. Prechter never registered as an investment adviser; he didn't need to. The typical subscriber is an interested investor who is already familiar with Elliott Wave Theory and wants to see what it indicates without working out its elaborate processes.

The investor theoretically makes his or her decisions on which stocks or bonds to buy on the basis of Prechter's analyses. Prechter wrote several books on Elliott Theory; a follower might need to master the jargon to know what his current report meant.

Prechter originally tracked the nine wave-degrees all the way back to the one that began in 1789. Using those waves, he then constructed the new ones into the original configuration to bring the chart up to date.

Prechter called the February 13, 1980, high of 903.34 to the day, but he was wrong in predicting a market decline that would last the rest of the year. In May he was calling for "a devastating crash for the summer of 1980"; it never came. He turned bullish in July.

"My performance there was very poor," he admits. "What shook me up was that the Dow indicators broke through, very briefly, a long-term, 40-year Elliott Support trendline. That was a false break. The only other false break of such a trendline that has ever occurred was in 1949. Even if it happened again, I'm afraid I'd have to go cautious. You can't buck a 40-year trendline."

For the rest of 1980, he did well. He called for a sell in August, when the Dow was at 960; it eventually went up to 1000.17 on November 20. The advance/decline line had turned negative in August. The advance to 1000.17 he termed a "sideways correction" that ended with the December 11 low.

In December 1980 the Elliott Waves told him the market was going up again. It did, reaching 1024.25 on April 27, 1981.

"I still am bullish. I don't think we've seen an intermediate top at all."

Soon enough he thought he had. "The markets are all spelling depression for sometime in the next ten years," he said in August 1982. Things were suddenly very bearish to Prechter. The weight of the technical indicators was forming evidence of a major depression by the late 1980s. There would be, he felt, a "very nasty market" by that time.

However, the good news was that there would be a "superbull market" before then.

"Investors have at least one fantastic ride in front of them. This last fling should run about five years and should leave the Dow peaking out at around the 3000 level."

In September 1982 he advised his followers to sell. The Dow was about 930. "There's no point in chasing a 150-point rally now, especially since I believe that there will be another good buying opportunity for investors in the fourth quarter."

There was, and he called it. Today, he's still looking forward to that "major depression" following his "superbull market" now in the making.

14
Richard Russell

Like C. Verne Myers, Richard Russell didn't start out as a market analyst or even on Wall Street. He began as a textile designer. But somewhere along the way he became interested in market trends and decided to try to figure out why they went where they did. He began devising his own theory of analysis, basing it on the earliest of them all—the C. H. Dow Theory.

Eventually he broke out in print with his bimonthly *Dow Theory Letters*. His newsletter was one of the first. "I've seen literally hundreds of letters come and go," he said.

Russell never confined himself, as did many of his colleagues, to the Dow 30 industrial average. Instead, he averaged in *all* the indexes—including transportation, utilities, and the composite average.

In addition, Russell looked over the characteristics of the stocks in the averages, including their yields, and calculated the ratios of advancing stocks to declining ones.

From this amalgam of information, he devised his own proprietary index—the Primary Trend Indicator—which he used to predict the turns of the market generally. Through the years, the PTI called various moves with an uncanny degree of accuracy.

Russell pointed out that the PTI was a coincident, not a leading, indicator. It was not capable, for example, of making the type of "turn-on-a-dime" call that other newsletter writers were so prone to make. Russell never intended to time his calls with sudden spurts or breaks in the market: "My experience of trading is that most people lose their shirts. The greatest use of the PTI is to avoid whipsaws, and go with the major underlying trend of the market."

Russell had no model portfolio to tout nor any special list of recommended stocks. In fact, he never liked to give advice at all on specifics: "What I really try to do is teach investing principles. I have a rather sophisticated bunch of readers. I don't say, 'Buy this,' or 'Do that,' the way a lot of services do. I give them alternatives and let them make up their own mind."

At least 7,000 people like it that way.

At the beginning of 1981, when the market was climbing in spite of very high interest rates, Russell sent his flock out of the market. Instead he put them into Treasury bills and gold.

"I've felt all along that with short-term interest rates so high, the risk/reward wasn't that fascinating in stocks. Anytime you can get absolute safety in T-bills at 14 or 15 percent or better, you're probably going to outperform most people in the market." And that included gold, although in the long run the market actually outperformed gold.

Had Russell followed his own PTI, he would have advised them differently. "It wasn't until well into the year [1980] that I began to trust the PTI. I thought it was going wrong."

As 1980 ended, Russell said that he thought there was a better than fifty-fifty chance that gold was going into a bear market.

"Gold hit 800 in January, dropped back, then went upward around 700. You've had tremendous inflation and political excitement since then, but now you have gold back to 625.10. I think gold is telling me what the spike in Treasury bond yields is: that the big squeeze in interest rates is on. They're going to hit this economy and hit it hard. There's been no distribution in gold in the last six months. If it breaks 600, there could be a panic on the downside."

Russell was worried about "the ultimate wind-down of the

greatest debt expansion in U.S. history," which had created an "inflate or die" mentality among Americans. Although he forecast "a huge accumulation pattern" in charts of Standard & Poor's list of 500 stocks, his preferred haven was still T-bills, then going at 13¼ percent.

"I don't think that anyone can predict what will hold up when it all hits the fan. In this kind of environment, the guy who loses least is the winner."

By October 1982 he was looking back over his shoulder at the new bear lows during August and wondering just what it all meant. He admitted that interest rates were beginning to stay down. The market had not really collapsed either. But it was still a bear market.

"We have, so to speak, a whole new ball game," he said. "The test of the primary trend happens after the initial rally off the lows. Once the rally is over, there will be a downward correction. If this correction holds above the previous lows, and the two average, then push above the preceding rally highs, a new bull market is signaled. But until and unless that happens, the primary trend remains in force."

By the end of November 1982, Russell had decided that perhaps the trend was going to be upward after all. In an advertisement published in Barron's on November 22, he was looking for a new high; the headline in the ad hinted at a breakthrough for the Dow in the 1200s.

He was right. The market began its upward march in November, with the final breakthrough into the 1200s on April 26, 1983, five months after his on-target prediction—on-target in spite of the fact that he hedged his statement about the Dow at 1200 with a question mark.

15
Stanley Weinstein

The editor of *The Professional Tape Recorder*, Stanley Weinstein, originally set up a system of market forecasting that included forty-four technical indicators. From an analysis of these indicators, he then compiled a semimonthly report that goes out to about 9,000 subscribers.

Weinstein's indicators are divided into three categories: *monetary, sentimental,* and *momentum.*

The monetary indicators usually show what the economy is doing in relation to the stock market and how it is affected, as well as how it is affecting, other countries.

The sentimental indicator shows the way people are viewing the stock market at the moment, computed from figures in odd-lot activity, retail cash, and margin-account trading and short-selling patterns.

The momentum indicator includes readings in the number of sales of shares and other dynamics of the stock market such as new highs and lows.

"A lot of guys follow indicator A or B, which work for a year or two, but then they foul up and they're in trouble. I use forty-four indicators with good track records and listen to the majority, so I'm not beholden to one or two."

In all, Weinstein is making his subscribers fairly happy.

"I do not claim to be infallible," he says. "But I make fewer mistakes than most, and when I do make a mistake I will correct it quickly." In contrast to the more flamboyant money gurus, Weinstein adds: "I do better than someone who says to buy or sell everything."

It was Weinstein who called the coming bull market in mid-July 1982. He gave his followers a buy order when the market was at 790. Those who followed him were lucky.

He later described how it felt to be all alone out there on the firing line calling for a bull market when the bears were taking potshots at him. "The market does whatever it has to do to confound the majority," he explained. "So when everyone expected the bear cycle to end with a bang, it went out with a whimper instead."

Weinstein recognized the end of the downturn and called for an upward movement. He was right. "The majority can be very right in the center of a move," he said. "It's at the turning point that they're usually grossly wrong. When I first predicted that the market would turn up in a very few weeks back in mid-July, I was a very lonely bull."

But he was a very correct bull.

In October he looked back at his move and described his feelings about the 1982 market. "It's the real thing. I know, everybody's concerned about Mexico and Poland. They're sure this is just a flash in the pan. But the bull market's for real. People just don't know how real it is."

But by the spring of 1983 they were beginning to get the idea.

16
Bert
Dohmen-Ramirez

Marketing his advice from Honolulu, Bert Dohmen-Ramirez established *The Wellington Financial Letter* some years ago, basing his forecasts on selected indicators. The service appears every month. In addition to the newsletter, he also sends out special bulletins; they are published once or twice a month at an extra cost.

Dohmen-Ramirez produces the monthly newsletter basically to make long-range predictions in the stock market. Readers who want short- or intermediate-range predictions are required to pay for the special bulletins. In fact, most of the recommendations do not appear in the monthly newsletter at all.

"Once a month is not enough," Dohmen-Ramirez explains. "If I see a stock that looks good, I don't want to have to wait a month to buy it. Also, we invest in these stocks for ourselves and our investment accounts. I don't want to be accused of first buying the stocks and then recommending them."

He usually bases his predictions on his own special considerations: "My theory states that liquidity in the financial system is the primary determinant of stock market directions. That works especially in this kind of volatile out-of-control environment, where there are frequent tight money–loose money periods."

He called the silver crash of March 27, 1980, which the Hunt brothers caused and which made the stock market plunge steeply: "Financial markets are now on the verge of collapse. The Federal Reserve has lost control of the situation, and if a banking crisis develops, it will not be able to stop it. Expect terrific washout, i.e., selling panic in all metals, commodities, bonds, stock market tomorrow, March 27, and March 28."

In August 1980 he predicted the market would go to 990–1020, but not before a consolidation phase. It hit 1000.17 on November 20, after moving through the 900s somewhat below 990.

He predicted that the Dow would be at 1050 in mid-January 1981 and that the high would be followed by a steep drop. The Dow hit 1004.69 on January 6, and then did drop.

17
William Donoghue

Inflation and the various ills it spawned during its first years of its domination of the U.S. economy resulted in sporadic attempts to control it. Several types of cures were suggested and tried; none proved immediately successful. One of the most efficacious but the one most reluctantly tried because of its painful aftereffects was a squeeze on circulating currency.

When the Federal Reserve Board began cutting down on the little inflationary puffs that were keeping the economy moving, the dollar became more valuable, especially to foreign financiers. As this happened, demand for it increased. And with the greater demand, the cost of using it rose; that translated immediately into higher interest rates.

High interest rates became the main problem of the U.S. economy, one that appeared on the horizon in the early 1970s. Corporations couldn't obtain money cheaply to invest in the future. When industry suffered, the stock market likewise ailed. The bond market deteriorated; high rates made bonds less and less attractive since they were long-term investments, and high interest prompted short-term loans.

There was a visible shift in the economy generally. One type of mutual fund quickly developed to take advantage of the immediate profit to be made in lending out large parcels of dollars in the money market. It was called a money market fund.

Within a few years, the money market funds almost swallowed

the entire mutual fund operation. In mid-1982 they were approaching the $200 billion mark, up from $10 billion at the end of 1978 and $74 billion at the end of 1980. Most of the money came from the nation's thrift institutions, regular mutual funds, and the stock market.

Such an enormous movement of money naturally attracted millions of new investors. The 165 money market funds competed with one another, and demanded someone to advise investors where to put their money.

And a guru did arise.

Originally an accountant, William Donoghue was floundering around as a CPA and as a financial consultant. After losing seven jobs in four years, he finally decided to return to Temple University to earn a masters degree in finance.

At Temple, in need of money to support his family, Donoghue began organizing seminars on corporate cash management. He also ran several seminars at Pennsylvania's Wharton School. That was in the mid-1970s, when the stock market was stumbling along and people weren't quite sure where to put their money.

At one of the Wharton seminars Donoghue met Daniel Butler, the publisher of a newsletter called *Butler's Money Fund Report.*

Money markets had started in 1971 as a type of "specialized" mutual fund: Bruce Bent had conceived the idea back in the early 1970s, and had failed to sell it to E. F. Hutton and Merrill Lynch. Bent then set up his own money fund with the then revolutionary idea of pooling investors' money in the money market itself rather than in the capital market, the capital market being the market consisting of stocks issued by corporations and bonds issued by public or private groups. The money market included securities issued by government agencies, large corporations, the Treasury Department. Since the sums of money borrowed were huge, they were issued on a short-term basis.

Bent began the Reserve Fund with $100,000 of his own money on November 5, 1971. Other money market funds were formed, but the idea didn't spread like wildfire. However, by 1974, when interest rates were zooming into the stratosphere, they did boom. Donoghue's friend Butler had started his newsletter to report on the funds and how much they were making for their investors. But rising interest rates had suddenly turned downward—a little pumping of money into the economy caused the drop—and by 1977 rates were at a nadir—if one can use the term.

Butler was looking for a buyer for his newsletter. Donoghue had a hunch about interest rates; he thought they might climb back up again. He paid Butler $14,000 for the newsletter and renamed it *Donoghue's Money Fund Report*.

William Donoghue was the man who was there at the right moment with the right product. As interest rates soared and the economy finally got used to the limp profits of the stock and bond markets, Donoghue's report showed people where they should be putting their money.

The public had never heard of the money market until Donoghue's report began to circulate. He started holding more seminars, not on cash management, but on the money market funds. Meanwhile he was refining his newsletter's capabilities. He supplied figures each week to his subscribers, showing exactly how much profit, or yield, each money market fund had made during the week—at least for the funds that sent him that information.

Donoghue determined the yields from these figures and published them on an annual basis, on a thirty-day basis, and on a seven-day basis. Some funds, including those run by Merrill Lynch, Pierce, Fenner & Smith and the Fidelity Group, refused to supply the seven-day figures, saying that such a short period was susceptible to too many distortions.

However, most others did. Donoghue continued to push for the money market funds in seminars, in appearances on television and radio, and in his weekly reports.

"When reporters call me, they know they're going to get a good quote," he once said. Each quote, of course, promoted the money market funds; Donoghue knew that his own success was dependent on theirs.

"He's a private entrepreneur trying to gain official status," grumbled one fund manager. He was branded a "promoter" and an "opportunist" by others in the field.

"I'm teaching people how to survive high inflation," he said in response to criticisms. And he proceeded to point out how people were being ripped off by savings banks that paid a maximum of 5½ percent. "Inflation is running at 12 and 13 percent," Donoghue warned. "People are losers to the banks!"

He admitted that there was a "friendly rivalry" between the money market funds and the savings banks. It was a competition the banks would have a hard time winning, he said, as long as their interest rates were so much lower. Money market fund rates were running 14 and 15 percent at the time. "Until that changes, I won't accept lower yields just so General Motors can get a lower prime."

When Congress lifted the interest-rate ceilings for banks and savings institutions, Donoghue wasn't too impressed. "I don't think the banks will ever conceive of a product that will truly compete with money funds. Banks can't offer investors the privilege of switching to alternate investments if interest rates drop. Money funds can do this and be in the right place at the right time. Money funds are in a position to move money faster."

Donoghue knew that there were risks in money fund investment: "But there's no way to make any money without some risk."

In 1981 Harper & Row published *William E. Donoghue's Complete Money Market Guide*. For many readers this was their first view of the phenomenon. The book not only enhanced Donoghue's reputation in the field of finance, but it brought in new subscribers to his newsletter.

Meanwhile the funds were growing by leaps and bounds, and Donoghue was charging $2,000 to run a seminar on the subject. Three of the biggest funds—Dreyfus Liquid Assets Fund, Midwest Income Investment Fund, and Capital Preservation Fund—were also using him to set up and appear at seminars.

His success of course spawned imitators. One of them was the National Association of Securities Dealers, which began putting out its own table of yield calculations for money market funds. They were slightly different from Donoghue's, but not appreciably so. Newspapers began printing both of the yield tables—one on Friday, for example, and the other on Sunday for the week's wrapup.

Donoghue's Money Fund Report comes from a tiny office in Holliston, Massachusetts—a four-room suite built over a general store. The door had no company name on it. Instead, the words P & S Publication Inc., appeared.

What did P & S stand for?

"Picks and shovels," Donoghue explained. "When all the world's out searching for gold, the thing to do is sell picks and shovels."

Donoghue's Picks and Shovels Report has made him the guru of the money market funds.

Assessment

To the great credit of the money messiahs portrayed in this book, they came through for the average investor at a time when traditional investment instruments—stocks and bonds—seemed to have played out their effectiveness for the time being. Their various suggestions offered a means of survival of sorts and protection when the stock market seemed to provide only losses and disappointment.

"All the old rules are not working," one unhappy investor said. "We're not being told where it's at."

But the messiahs did tell the world where it was at.

Even now they continue to offer alternatives to traditional investments. And because they offer advice that is available to the average person with some money to invest—advice as easily accessible as the lines in a newsletter—they can help almost anyone who wants to be helped. Their expertise covers many different investment facets, from the stock and bond markets, all the way over into the mutual funds, the money markets, and even gold, silver, strategic metals, and collectibles.

* * *

For example, Eliot Janeway, "the grand old man of the Cassandra circuit," as *Money* once described him, can be consulted for his general recommendations on the stock market. Janeway doesn't give explicit stock recommendations, but he does spot incipient trends and predicts rises in certain kinds of stocks.

In addition, he understands the interrelation between the global economy and stock market behavior. And he follows movements in other parts of the financial picture—for example, gold fluctuations, which he predicted accurately in 1975.

Because he is more of a general analyst than a technician or fundamentalist, Janeway can foresee major trends in the making, and his pronouncements on important themes like inflation, high interest rates, and stagflation bear watching, for he is usually right.

How these general movements will affect a particular stock or commodity is up to the investor to decide, not to Janeway. But he is *the* messiah to consult.

*   *   *

Joseph Granville is a man who frequently brags about followers who come up to him and say things like: "Mr. Granville, you made me a rich man." Granville's expertise is quite different from Janeway's. He makes people rich—when his advice works—by telling them exactly when to get into the market and when to get out.

Granville's particular genius lies in stock market analyses, in the way he adds up all the indicators and comes up with an answer that will in many cases parallel the movement that the market will soon make.

And, at times, Granville does actually call accurate turns when the market goes sharply up or down. Whether these factors cause the market to make the moves he predicted or whether he has simply made an astute and accurate forecast is not quite the point. The fact is that sometimes he is dead right—he *was* dead right in at least two important instances.

Granville's tendency to heavy show-business self-promotion and his overblown theatricality may annoy some, but his ability to spot market trends in advance cannot be scorned.

Timing is essential in following Granville. He himself works so fast that sometimes his followers are left in the dust, and consequently are trampled by the herd.

His very success turns some people against him. With Granville, it is essential to move quickly the moment he speaks.

*   *   *

John M. Templeton is a money messiah only in the sense that he is a financial leader of such consequence in the way he shops for stocks and manages his mutual funds that he should be consulted for advice from time to time.

The thing to do is to buy into a Templeton fund and let him do the work. His advice doesn't come out regularly in the form of a newsletter; he doesn't need to purvey counsel to anyone. His fund records speak for themselves.

For the investor who doesn't want to select individual stocks— one who doesn't want to consult seers like Janeway or Granville—the easy way out is to buy into one of the mutual funds and let the fund do the investing.

There are, of course, dozens of funds other than Templeton's. Each is involved in a unique portfolio that makes it function. One tool to better understanding the mutual fund market is the *Wiesenberger Report*, obtainable by subscription or at the library. This is a monthly publication recording the moves of all the mutual funds. The Weisenberger organization also provides a yearly book with explanations of the various funds and their performances over a ten-year period to establish the track record of a variety of funds.

Newspapers frequently interview Templeton because he is one of the best performers of all mutual fund managers in the accuracy of his selections. His words of advice are unusually apt at the time he gives them.

*   *   *

James Dines, the Original Goldbug, is basically a very good technical analyst, much like Granville, who has his own special formula for dealing with trends in the stock market and elsewhere.

Dines recommends stocks as well as other buys. He is not strictly committed to the stock market or the bond market and moves about in all areas of the financial world. For example, although he is a hard-money advocate, in 1974 he advised investors to stick to Treasury bills!

When gold was the big buzz word on the Street, Dines concentrated on it to a degree that tended to obscure his real accomplishments in predicting market trends. He is a better analyst than is generally believed.

* * *

Howard Ruff is really not a technical analyst of the stock market at all. In fact, in his newsletter, he spends less time with investment advice, both general and specific, than he does with other tips on how to live the right kind of life.

His obsession is with the approaching end of the world—at least the world as he sees it. He still insists that everyone should stock a year-and-a-half's supply of food in the house. And he believes that we will soon be bartering goods without any money or coinage at all to use.

Ruff likes to recommend diamonds and real estate rather than money or stocks. In fact, he has written off the stock market as too uncertain.

But he does dispense good advice on mores and life-styles, and he has been consistently right about the ravages of inflation and the seriousness of its unchecked domination of the economy.

Ruff has been changing from an exclusively doom-and-gloom approach to a more balanced sort of outlook. He reasons that in buying up gold and silver and burying it, the investor may retain the value of the metal, but in times of solid stock market rise, neither precious metal provides dividends or interest the way stocks do.

Ruff knows this. He is starting up other newsletters that will be in style if prosperity unexpectedly returns. He is a forward-looking prognosticator.

* * *

Douglas R. Casey, Harry Schultz, James Sinclair, Ian McAvity, Harry Browne, and C. Verne Myers all tend to be doom-and-gloomers. All blame inflation on government debasement of the currency. All say that big government is not the answer to monetary problems.

Some of their calls have been excellent. If government becomes less interfering, where will they go? No one knows.

* * *

The predictions of Martin Zweig, Robert Prechter, Richard Russell, Stanley Weinstein, and Bert Dohmen-Ramirez are based on painstaking analyses of the stock market and its performance. With the market neither in a sustained upward movement nor in a sustained downward trend, these short-term predictions can do a lot of good.

However, with the average investor wanting something that will give him a great deal more return than he might get from stocks and bonds, or gold and silver, where does he turn?

William Donoghue would say that he should try the money market funds.

Donoghue's weekly assessment of the yields of the money market funds is published in many newspapers. However, his weekly report contains much more detailed information. From this newsletter, the investor can make up his or her mind about specific funds, probably more accurately than by looking at a newspaper chart under "Donoghue."

* * *

Generally speaking, not all Wall Street analysts think much of the newsletters, which they accuse of running in packs—all pessimistic together or all optimistic together. With the current sentiment running mildly bearish in the newsletters, one analyst says: "This is a time to buy stocks. Historically, the market letters, of which there are about a thousand, usually are wrong."

With the market letters bearish, the sophisticated analyst then becomes bullish.

This might be called the rule of the Countercyclicity of Newsletters.

However, the "rule" doesn't take into consideration the many times the newsletter writers are all absolutely right.

One thing to remember about messiahs: they aren't omniscient, but they are correct an unusual amount of the time. And for that reason they usually deserve the large following they get.

Newsletters and Periodicals

Harry Browne

*Harry Browne's Special
   Reports*
One year.   10 issues $195.
PO Box 5586,
Austin, TX 78763

James Dines

The Dines Letter
One year.   12 issues $150.
PO Box 22,
Belvedere, CA 94920

Bert Dohmen-Ramirez

*The Wellington Financial
   Letter*
One year.   12 issues $195.
Hawaii Building,
745 Fort Street,
Honolulu, HI 96813

William Donoghue

*Donoghue's Money Fund
   Report*
One year.   52 issues $250.
Holliston, MA 01746

Joseph Granville

The Granville Market Letter
One year.   46 issues $250.
Drawer O,
Holly Hill, FL 32017

Eliot Janeway

The Janeway Letter
One year.   50 issues $250.
Janeway Publishing,
PO Box 2121,
Memphis, TN 38159

C. Verne Myers

*Myers' Finance & Energy
   Letter*
One year.   14 issues $200.
418 Peyton Bldg.,
Spokane, WN 92201

Ian McAvity

Deliberations
One year.   24 issues $150.
PO Box 182,
Adelaide St. Station,
Toronto, Ont., Canada
   M5C 2J1

Robert Prechter

The Elliott Wave Theorist
One year. 11 issues plus
    special reports $233.
New Classics Library,
PO Box 262,
Chappaqua, NY 10514

Howard J. Ruff

*Howard Ruff's Financial
    Survival Letter*
One year.   24 issues $145.
PO Box 2000,
San Ramon, CA 94583

Richard Russell

*Richard Russell's Dow Theory
    Letters*
One year.   26 issues $185.
PO Box 1759,
La Jolla, CA 92038

Harry Schultz

*The International Harry
    Schultz Letter*
One year. $258.
c/o Xebex,
PO Box 134,
Princeton, NJ 08540

Stanley Weinstein

The Professional Tape Reader
One year.   24 issues $250.
PO Box 2407,
Hollywood, FL 33022

Martin Zweig

The Zweig Forecast
One year.   18 issues $245.
747 Third Avenue,
New York, NY 10017